Ethics in Investment Banking

Also by Edmund Newell

WHAT CAN ONE PERSON DO? Faith to Heal a Broken World (*with Sabina Alkire*)

Ethics in Investment Banking

John N. Reynolds

with

Edmund Newell

First published 2011 by
PALGRAVE MACMILLAN

Palgrave Macmillan in the UK is an imprint of Macmillan Publishers Limited, registered in England, company number 785998, of Houndmills, Basingstoke, Hampshire RG21 6XS.

Palgrave Macmillan in the US is a division of St Martin's Press LLC, 175 Fifth Avenue, New York, NY 10010.

Palgrave Macmillan is the global academic imprint of the above companies and has companies and representatives throughout the world.

Palgrave® and Macmillan® are registered trademarks in the United States, the United Kingdom, Europe and other countries.

ISBN 978–0–230–28508–8

This book is printed on paper suitable for recycling and made from fully managed and sustained forest sources. Logging, pulping and manufacturing processes are expected to conform to the environmental regulations of the country of origin.

A catalogue record for this book is available from the British Library.

Library of Congress Cataloging-in-Publication Data
Reynolds, John N., 1966–
    Ethics in investment banking / John N. Reynolds with Edmund Newell.
        p.   cm.
    Includes index.
    Summary: "The financial crisis focused unprecedented attention on ethics in investment banking. This book develops an ethical framework to assess and manage investment banking ethics and provides a guide to high profile concerns as well as day to day ethical challenges"— Provided by publisher.
    ISBN 978–0–230–28508–8 (hardback)
    1. Investment banking—Moral and ethical aspects.   2. Business ethics.   I. Newell, Edmund.   II. Title.
    HG4534.R49 2011
    174'.4—dc23   2011028836

10   9   8   7   6   5   4   3   2   1
20   19 18 17 16 15 14 13 12 11

Printed and bound in Great Britain by
CPI Antony Rowe, Chippenham and Eastbourne

Contents

Preface

> The love of money is the root of all evil
>
> The First Letter of Paul to Timothy, chapter 6, verse 10

We have written this book primarily to assist investment bankers, stakeholders such as regulators and politicians, and those interested in starting an investment banking career in understanding how ethics can be applied in investment banking.

Since 2007, as the financial crisis has played out, there has been much criticism of investment banking and calls for more ethical behaviour by investment banks and investment bankers. At the same time, much of the commentary from outside the sector has been vague (such as trying to apply ethical principles without understanding what happens in an investment bank on a day-to-day basis), or it has been polemical (such as criticism of "speculation" without defining what is being criticised, and detailing what is wrong with it).

The financial crisis has shown that ethical failures can have profound consequences on the value of an investment bank and its reputation, and in our view investment banks have not taken ethics sufficiently seriously. Investment bankers typically have compulsory annual training in legal and regulatory compliance, but not in ethics; and although every major investment bank has a Code of Ethics, which sets requirements for ethical behaviour, these are of limited scope and have proved to be of little practical use.

This book does not focus on legislation, regulation and compliance (although all three are covered briefly where relevant). Our subject is ethics – and it needs to be stated clearly from the outset that, while ethics and compliance relate to one another, they are not the same.

Compliance, by definition, is concerned with complying with existing laws and regulations, and every investment bank has an established Compliance Department and sophisticated processes to ensure this happens. Ethics is broader, and is fundamentally about discerning what is right in a given situation – and acting on it.

There is naturally some blurring between the two: both compliance and ethics (when applied to business) are concerned with standards in doing business. However, whereas compliance is primarily concerned with a finite body of regulation and legislation and its applicability in business, ethics deals with the underlying nature, intention and result of a situation or action.

The reason for focusing on ethics is simple: every situation and action in investment banking (and in business as a whole) has ethical connotations, but many are outside areas governed by compliance. As a result, much business activity takes place without moral scrutiny. In practice, it is perfectly possible for an investment banker to structure a non-compliant deal to avoid a specific compliance problem, and in the process ignore any significant ethical questions that the deal raises. The financial crisis has exposed the dangers of this approach. Ethics, therefore, involves going beyond the legal requirements and rules imposed by regulatory bodies to determine what is right when making a business decision.

In *Ethics in Investment Banking* we set out a method for thinking about ethics in the industry, assess the ethical issues associated with areas of concern that have arisen from the financial crisis and are found more generally in investment banking, and look at the day-to-day ethical issues that investment bankers might face. Although the financial crisis has brought attention to bear on capital market activities, which is our main focus, we also cover advisory activities, making this book applicable both to integrated investment banks and to specialist firms.

At the end of each chapter we highlight what we believe are the main ethical issues facing investment banks, provide a chapter summary and pose a key question, which we hope will assist interested readers in honing their skills in applying ethical thinking. Towards the end of the book we provide a Quick Reference Guide for investment bankers to review contentious issues and their ethical implications. We conclude with a proposed framework for ethical conduct in investment banking, including proposing a new approach to producing a Code of Ethics and a recommendation for ethical self-regulation across the industry.

We are very grateful for the help and advice we have been given in producing this book. Our own ethical thinking has been sharpened by being members of the Church of England's Ethical Investment Advisory Group, and we would like to thank Deborah Sabalot for her insights into regulatory law, and Mark Bygraves, Sabina Alkire and Nigel Biggar for their comments on different aspects of the text.

Glossary

2 and 20: fee structure typically used by hedge funds whereby a 2 per cent base fee is levied on funds under management and 20 per cent of the upside or profit is paid

Abrahamic faiths: collective term for Judaism, Christianity and Islam, relating to their historic and theological origins

Adviser: an investment banking or financial adviser giving advice primarily related to valuation, assisting with negotiation, co-ordinating due diligence and project management

Agent: an investment bank trading in the market on behalf of a client and typically receiving a commission

AGM: the annual general meeting of a company

Arranger: individual or group, usually an investment bank, charged with arranging finance for a transaction. Arranging finance would consist of preparing presentations to potential funders and securing financing (normally debt, but this can also include additional sources of equity finance)

Bait and switch: investment banking practice of marketing a (senior) team of bankers to a client and then replacing them with more junior bankers once a mandate has been awarded

Big cap: a quoted company with a large market capitalisation or share value

Business ethics: an ethical understanding of business, applying moral philosophical principles to commerce

Capital markets: collective term for debt and equity markets; reference to the businesses within an investment bank that manage activity in the capital markets

Casino capitalism: term used to describe high-risk investment banking activities with an asymmetric risk profile

Categorical imperative: the concept, developed by Immanuel Kant, of absolute moral rules

CDS: credit default swap, a form of financial insurance against the risk of default of a named corporation

CEO: chief executive officer, the most senior executive officer in a corporation

Church Investors' Group (CIG): a group of the investment arms of a number of church denominations, mainly from the UK and Ireland

Code of Ethics: an investment bank's statement of its requirements for ethical behaviour on the part of its employees

Compensation: investment bankers' remuneration or pay

Compliance: structures within an investment bank to ensure adherence to applicable regulation and legislation

Conflict of interest: situation where an investment bank has conflicting duties or incentives

Corporate debt: loan made to a company

Credit rating: an assessment of the creditworthiness of a corporation or legal entity given by a credit rating agency

CSR: Corporate Social Responsibility

DCF: discounted cash flow

Debtor in Possession finance (DIP finance): secured loan facility made to a company protected from its creditors under chapter 11 of the US bankruptcy code

Derivative: a security created out of an underlying security (such as an equity or a bond), which can then be traded separately

Dharma: personal religious duty, in Hinduism and Buddhism

Discounted cash flow valuation: the sum of:

- the net present value (NPV) of the cash flows of a company over a defined timescale (normally 10 years);
- the NPV of the terminal value of the company (which may be the price at which it could be sold after 10 years); and
- the existing net debt of the company

Distribution: the marketing of securities

Dodd–Frank Act: the Dodd–Frank Wall Street Reform and Consumer Protection Act

Downgrade: a reduction in the recommended action to take with regard to an equity; or a reduction in the credit rating of a corporation

Duty-based ethics: ethical values based on deontological concepts

EBITDA: Earnings Before Interest Tax Depreciation and Amortisation

EIAG: the Ethical Investment Advisory Group of the Church of England

Encyclical: official letter from the Pope to bishops, priests, lay people and people of goodwill

Enterprise value (EV): value of an enterprise derived from the sum of its financing, including equity, debt and any other invested capital, which should equate to its DCF value

ERM: the European Exchange Rate Mechanism, an EU currency system predating the introduction of the euro

ETR: effective tax rate

EV:EBITDA: ratio used to value a company

Exit: sale of an investment

Free-ride: economic term for gaining a benefit from another's actions

Financial adviser: see Adviser

Glass–Steagall: the 1933 Act that required a separation of investment and retail banking in the US

Golden Rule: do to others as you would have them do to you

Hedge fund: an investment fund with a specific investment mandate and an incentivised fee structure (see **2 and 20**)

High yield bond: debt sold to institutional investors that is not secured (on the company's assets or cash-flows)

HMRC: Her Majesty's Revenue and Customs, the UK's authority for collecting taxes

Hold-out value: value derived from the contractual right to be able to agree or veto changes

Ijara: Shariah finance structure for project finance

Implicit Government guarantee: belief that a company or sector benefits from the likelihood of Government intervention in the event of crisis, despite the fact that no formal arrangements are in place

Initial Public Offering (IPO): the initial sale of equity securities of a company to public market investors

Insider dealing: trading in shares in order to profit from possessing confidential information

Insider trading: see Insider dealing

Integrated bank: a bank offering both commercial and investment banking services

Integrated investment bank: an investment bank that is both active in capital markets and provides advisory services

Internal rate of return (IRR): the annualised return on equity invested. Calculated as the discount rate that makes the net present value of all future cash flows zero

Investment banking: providing specialist investment banking services, including capital markets activities and M&A advice, to large clients (corporations and institutional investors)

Investment banking adviser: see Adviser

Islamic banking: banking structured to comply with Shariah (Islamic) law

Junior debt: debt that is subordinated or has a lower priority than other debt

Junk bond: see High yield bond

Lenders: providers of debt finance

Leverage: debt

Leveraged acquisition: acquisition of a company using high levels of debt to finance the acquisition

LIBOR: London Inter-Bank Offered Rate, the rate at which banks borrow from other banks

Liquidity: capital required to enable trading in capital markets

M&A: mergers and acquisitions; typically the major advisory department in an investment bank

Market abuse: activities that undermine efficient markets and are proscribed under legislation

Market capitalism: a system of free trade in which prices are set by supply and demand (and not by the Government)

Market maker: a market participant who offers prices at which it will buy and sell securities

Mis-selling: inaccurately describing securities (or other products) that are being sold

Moral hazard: the risk that an action will result in another party behaving recklessly

Moral relativism: the concept that morals and ethics are not absolute, and can vary between individuals

Multi-notch downgrade: a significant downgrade in rating or recommendation (by a rating agency)

Natural law: the concept that there is a universal moral code

Net assets: calculated as total assets minus total liabilities

Net present value (NPV): sum of a series of cash inflows and outflows discounted by the return that could have been earned on them had they been invested today

NYSE: New York Stock Exchange

Operating profit: calculated as revenue from operations minus costs from operations

P:E: ratio used to value a company where P (Price) is share price and E (Earnings) is earnings per share

Price tension: an increase in sales price of an asset, securities or a business resulting from a competitive situation in an auction

Principal: equity investor in a transaction

Principal investment: proprietary investment

Private equity: equity investment in a private company

Private equity fund: investment funds that invest in private companies

Proprietary investment: an investment bank's investment of its own capital in a transaction or in securities

Qualifying instruments: securities covered by legislation

Qualifying markets: capital markets covered by legislation

Quantitative easing: Government putting money into the banking system to increase reserves

Regulation: legal governance framework imposed by legislation

Restructuring: investment banking advice on the financial restructuring of a company unable to meet its (financial) liabilities

Returns: profits

Rights-based ethics: ethical values based on the rights of an individual, or an organisation

SEC: the Securities and Exchange Commission, a US regulatory authority

Sarbanes–Oxley: the US "Company Accounting Reform and Investor Protection Act"

Senior debt: debt that takes priority over all other debt and that must be paid back first in the event of a bankruptcy

Shariah finance: financing structured in accordance with Shariah or Islamic law

Sovereign debt: debt issued by a Government

Speculation: investment that resembles gambling; alternatively, very short-term investment without seeking to gain management control

Socially responsible investing (SRI): an approach to investment that aims to reflect and/or promote ethical principles

Spread: the difference between the purchase (bid) and selling (offer) price of a security

Subordinated debt: see Junior debt

Syndicate: group of banks or investment banks participating in a securities issue

Syndication: the process of a group of banks or investment banks selling a securities issue

Takeover Panel: UK authority overseeing acquisitions of UK public companies

Too big to fail: the concept that some companies or sectors are too large for the Government to allow them to become insolvent

Unauthorised trading: trading on behalf of an investment bank or other investor without proper authorisation

Universal bank: an integrated bank

Utilitarian: ethical values based on the end result of actions, also referred to as consequentialist

Volcker Rule: part of the Dodd–Frank Act, restricting the proprietary investment activities of deposit-taking institutions

Write-off: reduction in the value of an investment or loan

Zakat: charitable giving, one of the five pillars of Islam

1
Introduction: Learning from Failure

There has been significant criticism of the ethics of the investment banking sector following the financial crisis. This book aims to provide a framework for the investment banking sector to consider ethical issues and move beyond the current regulatory and compliance thinking that has dominated debates of "ethics" in investment banking.

Scrutiny of investment banking's role in the financial crisis has led to real questions being asked about the ethical basis of investment banking and the ethics of the capital markets on which much investment banking is based.

"Ethics" in moral philosophy, the sense in which we use it in this book, is the study of what actions and thoughts are right and wrong. Actions that are perfectly legal, but nonetheless unethical, can have profound implications for an investment bank, including severe reputational damage. The meaning of "ethics" is therefore wider than that of specific regulatory and legal codes relating to investment banking. Ethics in this broad sense is important to investment banking in the wake of the financial crisis. High levels of political and public concern about the sector will influence the level of independence and freedom that is politically acceptable, and will therefore affect profits and remuneration. As beneficiaries of enormous sums from Government intervention to support specific banks and therefore the capital markets as a whole, investment banks are now expected by politicians and the public to behave not only legally, but ethically – for it becomes a problem for investment banks if their expectations of ethical behaviour do not match those of politicians and the public.

Our definition of "investment banking" is based on the organisation and activities of investment banks, rather than on a strict regulatory or legal definition. By "investment banking", we are referring to the activities

carried out by the bulge bracket banks and other "integrated" investment banks (carrying out both capital markets and advisory activities),
the investment banking arms of "universal" banks (combining investment
banking and commercial/retail banking) and the activities of specialist
investment banks, who may carry out one or more of the investment
banking activities of the bulge bracket and integrated investment banks.
These include a range of capital markets activities (e.g., research, sales
and trading), advisory services such as M&A (mergers and acquisitions)
and other associated services, such as fundraising and "prime-brokerage"
(raising funds for private equity and hedge funds). Investment banking
typically also includes a range of specialised lending or investment activities, although investment banks' freedom to invest is increasingly limited
by regulation, notably the "Volcker Rule". This definition may not coincide in all respects with regulatory definitions of investment banking as
opposed to banking, but reflects what we believe to be the organisational
structure of, and services provided by, investment banks.

In the past, investment banks have paid insufficient attention to ethical
considerations, and it is unclear in the light of the financial crisis whether
this will, or can, substantially change. However, should it do so there is
uncertainty regarding where the focus should be. Debate about investment
banking ethics can be characterised as a clash between proponents of a
rights-based approach to investment banking ethics, and those who believe
that investment banking ethics are based on a series of duties. On the one
hand, an investment bank has a right to utilise its intellectual property, but
on the other it has duties of care to stakeholders – notably its clients – and,
as will be seen, these can conflict. We argue that investment banks should
not subjugate ethical duties to ethical rights, and to do so specifically risks
unethical behaviour.

Investment banks have been accused of major ethical failings, and the
political and popular perception is that the investment banking industry
is in need of reform but is unwilling and unable to reform itself. Investment banking has become subject to an unprecedented level of public
and political opprobrium and scrutiny. Legislation has been enacted in
many jurisdictions not only to increase regulation, but also to increase
taxes on banks and other financial institutions and limit remuneration,
especially that of directors and other senior management. Previous ethical failures by investment banks have proved to be costly: following the
dotcom crash, investment banks paid $1.4 billion in fines in the US,
resulting from securities violations, including fraud in the handling of
stock recommendations.

While investment banking may display attributes of "casino capitalism" (a term that will be considered later), it is nonetheless an intrinsic part of the modern economy, and provides essential services to Governments and corporations. Investment banks do not exist in a vacuum and therefore inevitably reflect ethical standards more generally prevalent in business. Investment banks have established client bases working with major companies, investment funds (such as private equity and hedge funds) and institutional investors, and also work closely with other professional services providers, notably lawyers.

Individual investment banks exist and succeed because (a) they offer services that are bought by clients, and/or (b) they trade effectively in the capital markets. In the case of all major investment banks, a significant proportion of their activities is, in some way, based on serving clients.

To some degree it is possible that in certain cases clients use investment banks because of, rather than in spite of, their ethical failings. For example, a client seeking to sell a business may wish to hire an investment bank that is prepared to break rules in order to conclude a deal on the best terms. Investment banking behaviour will inevitably reflect both wider prevailing standards of behaviour and also clients' (both corporate clients and institutional investors) demands.

It is also important to bear in mind that other sectors of the economy have also been faced with ethical problems, including bribery in the defence industry, encouraging potentially harmful sales of alcohol and tobacco in the retailing sector and mis-selling in the retail financial services sector. Raising ethical standards in investment banking is therefore part of a bigger picture and should not be seen in isolation. Investment banks work so closely with institutional investors and major industrial companies, as well as law firms, that the ethics of the investment banking sector are almost inevitably aligned to some extent with the standards of commerce and industry generally. Ethical failures in investment banking therefore probably reflect wider ethical concerns in business.

Despite many recent adverse political statements and press comments in relation to the financial crisis, there is no reason to assume that investment banking is especially – or intrinsically – unethical. Given the size of the investment banking sector, the transactions and trades in which investment banks are instrumental, and the influence that the sector wields on commerce and Government, the investment banking sector can be a major force for good. Nevertheless, the criticisms levelled at investment banking as a result of the financial crisis are legitimate, and many of them raise profound ethical issues.

Ethics and the financial crisis

The causes of the financial crisis are complex, but include ethical failings by investment banks (among others). The US Financial Crisis Inquiry Commission blamed failures in regulation; breakdowns in corporate governance, including financial firms acting recklessly; excessive borrowing and risk by households and Wall Street; policymakers ill-prepared for the crisis; and systematic breakdown in accountability and ethics.[1] The UK's Independent Commission on Banking cited factors including "global imbalances, loose monetary policy, light-touch regulation, declining under-writing standards, widespread mis-pricing of risk, a vast expansion of banks' balance sheets, rapid growth in securitized assets".[2]

The UK economist Roger Bootle diagnosed the crisis in a more straightforward way in his 2009 book *The Trouble with Markets*: "greedy bankers and naive borrowers, mistaken central banks and inept regulators, insatiable Western consumers and over-thrifty Chinese savers".[3] Others have also directly cited bankers' greed. Gordon Brown, the UK Prime Minister at the time the financial crisis developed, in his book examining the financial crisis, *Beyond the Crash*, has blamed "excessive remuneration at the expense of adequate capitalisation" for the UK banking crisis.[4]

It is clear that incentives in the form of the high levels of pay received by investment bankers creating and trading seriously flawed products was a contributing factor to the financial crisis. The asymmetry of risk and reward in investment bankers' remuneration can incentivise risk-taking: there is an opportunity to be paid very well if a trade is profitable, but the investment banker does not actually lose money (in the form of cash – the value of any equity owned in the investment bank can reduce) if a trade is loss-making. However, despite the criticisms of investment bankers' "greed", we do not find it compelling to base the blame for the financial crisis on greed alone or as the major contributor to the crisis.

Many investment bankers would accept that a desire to personally make large amounts of money is one of their driving forces. However, this does not necessarily equate with "greed", which can be defined as the desire to acquire or consume something beyond the point of what is desirable or can be well used. While we cannot determine the motives behind an individual's pursuit of wealth, the high levels of remuneration in investment banking raise the question of whether there is such a thing as "institutional greed". In a highly competitive industry where long-term employment is not guaranteed and where, because of the heavy work demands, careers can be short, there is an incentive for investment bankers to make as much money as quickly as possible. Whether or not that can be construed as greed or as a sensible strategy in terms of potential lifetime earnings is unclear.

One of the results of the financial crisis was that some investment bankers who had accumulated substantial equity holdings in their employers saw this wealth almost entirely obliterated. Many senior investment bankers (including the CEOs of Lehman and Bear Stearns, two of the high-profile investment banks to fail during the crisis) themselves lost considerable sums during the crisis. Were they the victims of their own – or institutional – greed? Opinions differ.

A consequence of greed is that it can cloud judgement and rational thinking. This is important in the context of the financial crisis as it has been argued that greed led to investment bankers taking undue risks. There is some validity in this, as it is unquestionably the case that risks were taken and investment bankers were incentivised by remuneration to take risky decisions. However, other factors were at play as well – including inaccurate credit ratings that greatly underestimated the risk associated with what proved to be "toxic" financial products.

Interestingly, among the proposed (and legislated) solutions to the financial crisis is a requirement for investment banking bonuses to be paid largely in equity (in the bankers' employers). Ownership of equity by investment bankers is, however, a practice that has been common for a considerable time – it has been common for a proportion of bonuses to be paid in "deferred equity" (equity vested over a period of, say, three years, dependent on the employee still being employed at the date of vesting). Ownership of very substantial amounts of equity by investment bankers, including ultimate decision-makers at investment banks most affected by the crisis, does not appear to have made an impact on the behaviour leading to the crisis. This appears to contradict the assertion that the crisis was based mainly on greed. Even if it is difficult to accept greed as the main cause of the financial crisis, whichever approach to understanding the crisis is accepted, it is clear that a part of the cause relates to a failure in investment banking ethics.

Investment banks have received an economic free-ride, based on an implicit guarantee that financial markets will receive Government support, as well as practical intervention by the state. This may impose ethical "duties" on investment banks (we will go on to define what an "ethical duty" is). The question of the nature of the ethical duties imposed on an investment bank in return for implicit Government backing of both banks and investment banks has now become important, even though the banking sector is clearly not the only one to benefit from such a guarantee. The scope of the implicit guarantee is not clear, for three reasons: first, because Lehman was allowed to fail, second, because new legislation and taxes have reduced its benefit and, third, because other sectors also benefit from implicit guarantees. The situation is further confused, and the extent of implied ethical duties potentially affected, by the contribution made to the financial crisis by regulatory failure. Nonetheless, the activities and behaviour of investment banks across a variety of areas are now subjects of public concern and political scrutiny and intervention. Bankers' remuneration (or compensation) is now a major political issue, and public and ethical concern about "inequitable" rewards received by investment bankers shows no sign of abating.

One lesson of the financial crisis has been that strictly legal behaviour, where it has ethical flaws, may nonetheless damage institutions, their employees and their shareholders. Actions may, while being strictly legal, also be plainly unethical. Pope Benedict XVI, in his encyclical *Caritas in Veritate* states that "Every economic decision has a moral consequence."[5] Equally, legal restrictions may exist for specific (perhaps political) reasons, and restrict activity that may otherwise be ethical.

Ethics has both a secular and a religious tradition. Ethics goes beyond legality, and may presage future laws or reflect public expectations of behaviour. In developing ethical thinking in investment banking, it is worth considering that where there are shared ethical concerns across the world's major religions, a significant proportion of the world's population shares a common view regarding the ethical value of actions. We have therefore made a specific analysis of sector-specific investment policies of five major faiths. Given the number of people professing these faiths (estimated at around 5 billion people), arguably such policies could provide a guide to economic involvement that would be ethically unacceptable to many cultures, even if not illegal. The growing importance of Islamic banking is indicative of this.

By behaving ethically, in addition to following relevant legal and compliance requirements, investment bankers and investment banks may protect their careers, shareholders and, in some extreme cases, their freedom. Ethical behaviour, although it would have helped avoid a number of the problems of the financial crisis, would probably not have obviated those issues relating to management capabilities and failings.

Regulation, legislation and, therefore, compliance are generally responsive to market developments. Given the speed of innovation in the capital markets and investment banking, this can mean that a prescriptive approach to ethics – following compliance rules – does not protect against unethical decisions or actions, which can then have damaging effects. An understanding of ethical principles may therefore have a specific value in protecting reputational and shareholder value.

Although investment banks claim to require ethical behaviour, empirical and anecdotal evidence very much contradicts this. Existing investment banking Codes of Ethics are, in practical terms, ineffective, and serve in the main to protect shareholders from abuse by employees, rather than protecting clients. Ethics and ethical behaviour should be inculcated throughout an investment bank, and not left to the realms of Compliance or Corporate Social Responsibility (CSR) departments, or as the prerogative of senior executives, often at a significant distance from front-line bankers.

Behaving ethically could result in an investment bank forsaking opportunities to take on profitable business. For example, an investment bank might decline to lead the Initial Public Offering (IPO) of a company if it did not "believe" in its long-term prospects, even if there was sufficient market demand to complete an initial offering. This could become a vicious circle, and result in the decline of the investment bank. Consequently, a form of strengthened outside regulation is also required in order to make ethical behaviour more general within investment banking.

Many of the constituent failings leading to the financial crisis were not novel. In its announcement of charges against Goldman Sachs in relation to the marketing of the financial product ABACUS, the US Securities and Exchange Commission (SEC) stated: "The product was new and complex but the deception and conflicts are old and simple"[6] – pointing to the repeated nature of failings identifiable in the financial crisis.

Some of the issues highlighted by the financial crisis, such as unauthorised trading or mis-selling securities, are clearly ethical in nature. A number of practices criticised for being unethical, such as short-selling, are more complex. The ethics of these practices are not simple or straightforward. For example, we would conclude that short-selling is not in itself normally unethical, but that it can be abused and become unethical. We also question the characterisation of "speculation" as unethical, and have difficulty separating it from other normal investment activities (see Chapter 6).

The scope of ethical issues

Understanding ethics in investment banking is not just about the major abuses identified in high-profile scandals. Individual investment bankers face specific ethical issues as part of their day-to-day activities. These can involve dealing with client-facing areas such as conflicts of interest or presenting misleading information in a pitch, as well as internal issues such as promotion and compensation decisions, misuse of resources and management abuses. Many of these issues can be relatively minor, but, nonetheless, how they are dealt with will be crucial in inculcating ethical decision-making within an investment bank.

When investment banks behave unethically, there can be significant consequences, including making losses or incurring fines. It can also involve criminal cases against individual bankers. Daniel Bayly, Merrill Lynch's former head of investment banking, received a 30-month prison sentence for his role in a trade by Enron involving Nigerian barges, aimed at misrepresenting Enron's earnings.

There have been cases where relatively junior investment bankers have received criminal or civil penalties for their involvement in illegal activities. By contrast with the sentence received by Mr Bayly, William Fuhs, a Vice President (a mid-level banker) at Merrill Lynch was sentenced to a longer period of custody – over three years. *The New York Times* described Mr Fuhs' role as "a Sherpa" on the deal (a "Sherpa" carries luggage for mountaineers, and this implies that Mr Fuhs' role was not a leading one).[7] As the case of Jamie Olis, an accountant at Dynegy, showed, sentencing guidelines based on calculations of the level of losses resulting from fraudulent activities can lead to lengthy prison sentences – the original sentence given to Mr Olis was a 24-year prison term (reduced to 6 years on appeal) in relation to a $300 million accounting fraud.

This underscores the importance for investment bankers at all levels to be able to raise legitimate questions about the ethics of what they are being asked to do – both to have a forum to raise questions, and to understand when it is necessary to do so. In extreme cases, the impact of unethical decisions can be very painful.

Ethics and performance

There are opposing views as to whether ethical behaviour helps or hinders performance in banking and investment banking. The author and former banker Geraint Anderson (also known as CityBoy), in an article entitled "This Godless City" concluded that it is harder for a religious person to succeed in "the City": "Well, thank God I used to be an atheist! I succeeded in the City precisely because I had no such ethical reservations restricting my hideous ambition."[8] The position of Stephen Green, the widely respected former Chairman of HSBC, who had previously run HSBC's investment bank (and who subsequently became the UK Government trade minister), would appear to contradict this statement – Mr Green is also an ordained minister in the Church of England. Ken Costa, who was Vice Chairman of UBS Investment Bank and subsequently Chairman of Lazard International is also Chairman of Alpha International, an evangelical Christian organisation.

The incentives, both financial and ethical, for senior level investment bankers can be different from those at more junior levels: senior level bankers may have more financial independence, providing a cushion against decisions that would adversely affect their remuneration; however, at the same time they may stand to be better rewarded from a profitable but unethical decision. In a capital markets business it is often the mid-level and less well-off bankers who are driven to produce the revenue. Interestingly, it is often the converse in an advisory business, where the senior bankers have almost exclusive contact with clients and must wrestle with any ethical issues relating to decisions on whether and how to execute transactions.

Investment banking has a distinct culture and distinct values: a culture that requires the highest levels of dedication, and equally high standards of analysis and deal execution. Investment banks profess (and normally display) corporate values including client service, dedication and innovation, which are frequently listed in advertisements. We believe that it is at least arguable that a major shift in ethical behaviour should be introduced very carefully so as not to undermine the capabilities of an investment bank in areas such as innovation and client service. Investment bankers often profess, more or less openly, personal values, including a desire to make money (which might be driven by "greed"), intense competitiveness and arrogance. These "values" do not easily accord with recognised ethical "virtues". However, it is not clear that if these values, when channelled constructively, have to be damaging to an investment bank or its clients. For example, the desire to personally make large amounts of money is not necessarily socially destructive. Some investment bankers describe making money as "a way of keeping score". Some have started charitable trusts and are active philanthropists. These personal values, which appear less frequently (if at all) in investment banks' advertising, in comparison to the more publicly acceptable corporate values (client service, dedication and so on), are also a part of investment banking culture, but are ones that, if not channelled appropriately, can be damaging.

We do not believe that adoption of an ethical framework for decision-making need undermine the core cultural values that make an investment bank successful, in the same way that legal restrictions on formerly acceptable practices such as insider dealing have not caused the decline of the investment banking sector. Inculcating ethical values into an investment banking culture will not be simple, but should be feasible given real management determination. As a starting point, investment banks should now be prepared to accept that a new approach to ethics is necessary to protect against damage caused by morally dubious transactions, and to reduce the need for extraneous influences reducing the scope for independent decision-making.

We would argue strongly that it is in the interest of the investment banking sector to place a new and practical emphasis on ethics, to train investment bankers to understand ethics and behave ethically, to include ethical behaviour in annual reviews, to identify ethical problems and to resolve them effectively. Investment banks need to show that they can genuinely inculcate ethical behaviour, partly in order to reduce outside intervention, which will otherwise impose restrictions on activities, profits and compensation.

Investment banks lack key tools to enable them to act and think ethically. Existing Codes of Ethics are, in practical terms, ineffective and should be radically revised. In addition, the investment banking sector could significantly enhance the prospects of both practically improving sector ethics and being seen by regulators and politicians to do so. One important method of achieving this would be to establish a sector-wide investment banking ethics committee, to enable ethical issues to be dealt with for the investment banking sector as a whole (as we set out in Chapter 9).

Ethical implications for investment banks

- The behaviour of investment banks is now the subject of intense political, media and public concern. Addressing ethical issues will assist in assuaging this concern and reduce intervention in the investment banking sector.
- Investment banks have received some form of economic free-ride, which imposes an enhanced ethical duty to support the Government.
- A change in behaviour, guided by more ethical concerns, would not resolve problems caused by management failures.

- Investment banks do not exist in a vacuum, and ethical standards reflect those standards generally prevalent in business.
- Behaving ethically could result in an investment bank losing opportunities to win profitable business. Some form of outside "regulation" is required as well as an internal determination to change investment banks' behaviour.
- Incentives, both financial and ethical, differ for senior bankers and for junior bankers.

Chapter summary

- Scrutiny of investment banking's role in the financial crisis has led to real questions being asked about the ethical basis of investment banking.
- Legislation has been enacted in many jurisdictions not merely to increase regulation, but also to increase taxes and limit remuneration.
- While investment banking may display attributes of "casino capitalism", it is an intrinsic part of the modern economy.
- Investment banks do not exist in a vacuum and so reflect standards of business ethics more generally prevalent. Other industries have also been faced with ethical problems.
- By behaving ethically, in addition to following relevant legal and compliance requirements, investment bankers and investment banks may protect their careers, shareholders and, in some extreme cases, their freedom.
- Investment banking has a distinct culture and distinct values: a culture that requires the highest levels of dedication, and equally high standards of analysis and deal execution.
- We do not believe that adoption of an ethical framework for decision-making would undermine the core cultural values which make an investment bank successful.
- Investment banks need to show that they can genuinely inculcate ethical behaviour in order to reduce outside intervention, which will otherwise impose restrictions on activities, profits and compensation.

Are investment banks right to (i) follow the law, and rely on law-makers to determine what is ethical; or (ii) should they set their own ethical standards?

2
Business Ethics and the Financial Crisis

Business ethics and market capitalism

The moral basis of how business should be conducted has been a matter of concern since antiquity. Yet the academic discipline of business ethics is relatively new, developing primarily over the last quarter of a century or so. A major impetus for business schools – and indeed businesses – to turn their attention to ethics was a spate of financial scandals in the late 1980s, which exposed the problem of "insider trading" in Wall Street, when the activities of Ivan Boesky, Michael Milken and others captured international headlines. Here was an issue of moral judgement – whether to use privileged information for personal gain – that caused public outcry and raised questions about the trustworthiness of employees and the way firms conducted their business.

Since then a number of high-profile and highly damaging incidents have also raised ethical concerns over finance. These include the liquidation of the Bank of Credit and Commerce International (BCCI) amid allegations of fraud; the bankruptcies of Enron and WorldCom, which were associated with "creative accounting" – the deliberate manipulation of accounts to obscure the true financial position of these firms – and also with fraud; the activities of rogue trader Nick Leeson, which brought about the collapse of Barings Bank, the UK's oldest merchant bank; Robert Maxwell's alleged misappropriation of the Mirror Newspaper Group's pension fund; the German FlowTex scandal, where non-existent machinery had been sold; and the Credit Lyonnais crisis in the early 1990s, following a disastrous expansion strategy and a failure of risk controls.

Although there has been media and political criticism of aspects of the behaviour of hedge funds and private equity funds, there does not seem to be any systematic evidence that the staggering growth of these sectors over the past two decades has presaged a decline in ethical standards in business. Scandals of the 1980s and 1990s pre-dated in many ways the growth of private equity and hedge funds and the widespread use of highly incentivised fee structures, such as the typical hedge fund 2 + 20 fee arrangements (2% management fee + 20% of the upside).

Nevertheless, the recent financial crisis has also raised new questions of an ethical nature. Whereas the instances just cited concerned the deliberate or alleged wrongdoing of management and individuals, the financial crisis exposed systemic issues within banking with an ethical dimension, which even called into question the moral basis of market capitalism.

The underlying view of this book is that there is nothing intrinsically ethical or unethical about market capitalism in general or investment banking in particular. However, markets, we believe, are not (as some argue) moral-free zones. Like any other institution, markets can operate or be influenced for good or ill, and for the benefit of some and to the detriment of others. What determines the ethics of a market are (a) the institutions that enable a market to fulfil its particular purpose, (b) the rules and legislation by which the market operates, and (c) the values and behaviour of market participants.

It is generally accepted that markets provide the most efficient economic system to facilitate economic growth through wealth creation. In an ethical sense this is a "good" – a desirable objective as it enables humans to flourish. Markets are conventionally seen as offering benefits to all users by providing for fair or best pricing to be achieved, and by having a high level of transparency so that informed and fair decisions can be made. The benefits of markets are readily apparent across the globe today. The improvement in the standard of living in many societies is a direct consequence of wealth creation enabled by market capitalism. There is evidence for this following the collapse of Communism in Eastern Europe in the 1980s and 1990s, with the transformation of former state-controlled "command" economies to market-based economies. Similarly, the recent emergence of rapidly developing countries such as China, India and Brazil demonstrates the impact of effective markets and capital investment. Without them, such transformation would not be possible – hence the growing impetus to look for market-based responses to those parts of the world blighted by extreme poverty.

Yet wealth creation brings with it social costs, such as global warming and its effect on the lives of many through rising sea levels, flooding and droughts – hence the attempts to find market-based (as well as other) solutions to that problem, such as emissions trading. As with so many things, there are positive and negative elements to market capitalism. Markets enable participants to exercise freedom of choice and encourage and reward effort, but they can also incentivise selfish attitudes and behaviour, and greed. Similarly, while markets distribute resources effectively, they can also distribute them in ways that cause high degrees of inequality. Exposure to national or international market forces can also change the nature of local economies resulting in, for example, the collapse of traditional industries or agriculture, or small independent shops. Here, too, moral questions are raised.

An important ethical consideration, therefore, is the type of market concerned. An unfettered labour market, for instance, could create extreme inequalities, leaving those at the lower end living in poverty, and so there is an argument for such a market to be regulated with minimum wage legislation. Within other markets, it could be argued that minimum intervention and maximum openness is desirable to ensure the most efficient allocation of resources (as has been argued in relation to free trade). A market that operates in an inefficient or dysfunctional way, either because of the way it is structured or because of the negative influence by key players, is a concern. This was understood by no less a figure than Adam Smith, who is regarded by many as the founding father of free-market economics through his great work *The Wealth of Nations*.[1] Smith makes clear, however, the dangers of potential market abuse as people pursue selfish ends. It is noteworthy, therefore, that Smith's other great (and earlier) work, *The Theory of Moral Sentiments*,[2] is about moral philosophy. Different markets raise different issues, including ethical ones. The issues raised by financial markets is a theme explored in this book.

Why investment banking is necessary

Investment banks are a product of market capitalism and utilise money and other markets to carry out a range of essential activities to support the economy. They have evolved from within and outside the banking system and have four main functions: (a) to raise capital required for investment both for companies and Governments, (b) to provide liquidity for markets to function effectively through trading in equity, debt and hybrid products, (c) to provide a wide range of beneficial financial services to the public and private sector, including research and advice on transactions, and (d) to create financial instruments designed to satisfy a market need (including the reduction of market volatility).

In terms of advisory and capital market activities, the investment banking sector has established itself and grown into a major global industry on the basis of fulfilling a market need for its services. Raising capital and managing financial risk are essential for corporations and Governments. On a different scale, the same type of services are necessary for individuals, where mortgage providers and Financial Advisers may carry out similar activities. In most cases, the services provided by investment banks are either so specialist or require such a major marketing (distribution) or trading capability – or both – that the cost of even Governments providing them are prohibitive. Put simply, investment banking is necessary to the modern economy because it enables businesses and Governments to fund themselves, and to do so in the most efficient way possible.

In addition, many investment banks take principal positions (that is, they make investments) either as a specific investment strategy for themselves or to facilitate client business. This is also a major driver for profitability – and for some investment banks it has become the major source of profits. The opportunity to benefit from market presence and understanding has helped many investment banks grow significantly, and some have groups, engaged in proprietary trading, that are remunerated and behave in a very similar way to hedge funds. This activity is not in any way novel for investment banks, although the balance of activities has changed considerably over time.

From an ethical perspective, capital market activities and fulfilling market demands for services can be seen as potentially beneficial: facilitating commerce, encouraging market efficiency and providing essential services on more or less competitive terms. As an investment activity, proprietary (or principal) investment may be regarded in itself as ethically neutral (although what is invested in may have ethical implications). Similarly, there is nothing intrinsically ethical or unethical about a business focused on investing in and trading financial instruments – although this type of activity is sometimes called "speculation", a term that has negative moral connotations. The ethics of speculation will be considered later.

Ethical problems and the financial crisis

Despite their strategic importance to the economy, investment banks have faced hostility and come under particular scrutiny during the recent financial crisis, in which three of the largest and best-known went out of business. The collapse of Lehman Brothers in September 2008 sent shock waves around the world and proved to be the tipping point of the "credit crunch", which also saw the fall of Bear Stearns (acquired by JP Morgan with US Government support) and Merrill Lynch (which was bought by the Bank of America).

During the financial crisis and in its aftermath, commentators, the press and politicians highlighted a series of shortcomings common across a number of investment banks. These can be summarised briefly as a combination of management failure, greed and *hubris* – the Greek term for when people believe they have god-like qualities. More specifically, the main criticisms levelled at investment banks in relation to the financial crisis are:

- They took undue risks in order to satisfy the greed of investment bankers.
- They failed to recognise the risks of their activities on the economic system as a whole, as well as the resulting human costs.
- They engaged in speculative "casino capitalism", akin to gambling.
- They created complex financial instruments that served no productive purpose other than to make money for the investment banks, while losing money for their clients.
- They remunerated staff at levels that were deemed inequitable and which provided strong incentives for excessive risk-taking.

As a result, there have been strong calls to separate investment and retail banking, so that the savings of the public at large are not exposed to high levels of risk – and perhaps also to place some distance between what the public perceives to be two morally distinct banking sectors: "utility" commercial and retail banks, and "casino" investment banks.

The reality is, inevitably, more complex. Although there were clearly management and ethical failings in investment banks, many lessons learnt from the crisis relate to sales of mortgages to retail customers, banking regulation and to managing counterparty risk. Attention has been focused on ethical decision-making at investment banks, notably the SEC's legal action against Goldman Sachs: on 16 April 2010, the SEC charged Goldman Sachs with fraud over the marketing of ABACUS-AC1, a sub-prime mortgage product (Goldman settled the case without admitting or denying wrongdoing).[3]

A number of different activities of investment banks have come under scrutiny following the financial crisis (see Chapter 6), including the mis-selling of securities. One of the central issues of the financial crisis was the development and sale of a huge volume of mortgage-backed securities by investment banks. These securities have become a focus of public, political and media concern. For example, Senator Levin, at the Senate Permanent Subcommittee on Investigations hearings into ABACUS-AC1, raised a series of ethical questions, including the duty of care of investment banks to clients, and whether investment banks should sell products in which they do not believe.

Much of the financial crisis was not novel

It is also worth looking back at previous banking crises to assess how much of the recent crisis is novel, and whether there are ethical implications for investment banks. A number of the areas of concern in the credit crunch were clearly understood to be existing problems from previous crises:

- The unreliability of credit ratings, including multi-notch downgrades and allegations of conflicts on interest was a major area of concern in the wake of the Enron and WorldCom credit downgrades and bankruptcies in 2001–2. These bankruptcies were not alone, as there was a series of failures in both the telecoms/cable and the independent power producer sectors. Governments failed to appropriately increase the effectiveness of oversight of credit rating agencies in the wake of the failures of Enron, WorldCom and so on.
- Sovereign debt crises and defaults are nothing new. Looking back to Latin America in the 1980s and early 1990s, and also at the impact of financial crises in major economies, such as the Russian banking crisis in 1997 or the UK in the 1970s, sovereign debt even in relatively stable countries has periodically exhibited relatively high levels of risk. Given the nature of a sovereign country, and its responsibilities (providing services such as health care, defence, education) for and from (e.g., tax raising) its citizens, the ethical position of trading in sovereign debt may have different characteristics than trading in corporate debt.
- Strategies involving short-selling are not novel. George Soros was shorting the pound when he famously profited from the UK's attempt to remain in the European Exchange Rate Mechanism (ERM) in 1992.
- The proximate cause of the credit crunch – mis-selling of high-risk mortgages in the US – is reminiscent of other mis-selling problems in the past, such as the IPO of some dotcom stocks and the sale to retail customers of endowment plans in the UK, although the economic damage from the sub-prime crisis was significantly greater than in previous cases.

The positive impact of investment banking

Although investment banking has received much recent criticism, it has also made positive contributions to society both directly and indirectly. It has done so directly, through enabling efficient financing from capital markets, and in "soft" areas such as encouraging meritocracy; it has contributed indirectly through the philanthropic activities of a number of investment bankers, as well as from the benefit of taxes paid (on the assumption that state use of taxes is beneficial).

The efficiency of markets is generally recognised as being beneficial to society, even though there are currently increased concerns about the adverse impact of dysfunctional markets. Arguments can be made about the role of regulators versus investment banks in ensuring efficient market operation, but it must be to the long-term benefit of investment banks as a sector that markets should operate effectively. There are cases where individual investment banks, or investment bankers, have profited disproportionately from inefficient markets, but this does not invalidate the argument that banks rely on, and benefit from, efficient and orderly markets.

Many investment banks have philanthropic programmes, although these are typically very limited in monetary size and scope. At the same time some investment banks actively encourage philanthropy or community work among their employees. The beneficial impact of investment banks could be significantly greater: it is surprising how relatively modest an impact the Canary Wharf development has had on some of the surrounding communities in the London Borough of Tower Hamlets, a borough that still ranks as among the poorest in the UK.

Regulation and regulatory changes

Investment banking regulation is based primarily on different national frameworks. In major markets, regulation of banks is highly complex, and covers most areas of investment banking in some form. Regulation, and compliance with regulations by investment banks, has become very prescriptive, based on specific detailed sets of rules or legislation. Investment banks typically work hard to comply with applicable laws and regulation. Such compliance can be very focused on specifically obeying individual rules, rather than in applying the spirit of the rules, even where the regulatory and compliance rules have themselves been based on broad principles.

In the 1990s there was a major industry-wide exercise in bringing about the repeal of Glass–Steagall, a highly influential regulatory change affecting banks in the US, the largest market for investment banking services. This act enforced the separation of investment and commercial banking, and was instigated in 1933 after the Wall Street Crash. The Financial Services Modernization Act repealed Glass–Steagall in 1999, allowing the mergers of different types of financial services companies; more specifically it allowed the merger of Citigroup with Travellers (an insurance company). There does not appear to have been a similar subsequent widespread call from investment banks to radically reduce or repeal regulation over recent years.

Self-regulation and the impact of legislation

Ethical issues within a company or industry can be addressed through outside regulation, via Government legislation and/or some form of enforcement by a regulatory body, or by self-regulation (also known as self-policing). Self-regulation can be seen, for example in the legal profession, in the US by the American Bar Association, and in the UK by the Law Society and the Bar Council. In some sectors, self-regulation has been advocated by companies, but is seen to have failed (either systemically or periodically). Where business practices are of public interest, and there is a political will to regulate, change in behaviour can sometimes be brought about more effectively by external regulation. In investment banking, where it is likely that a highly ethical stance would, in the short term, result in a competitive disadvantage, there is an argument that major change may be more likely to be brought about by external regulation via legislation and enforcement. For example, section V of the Goldman "Business Standards Report" states that the firm's disclosure should not competitively disadvantage it.[4] **In a highly competitive industry such as investment banking, self-regulation is unlikely to bring about a change in ethical values without outside impetus, either through legislation and/or regulation or alternatively through industry-wide co-operation.**

Compliance

Compliance is firmly embedded in investment banking and is generally managed effectively. However, although some banking regulation is supposedly principles-based, in practice it is primarily a process-driven function of complying with the law and regulations, and does not normally enter into an ethical debate on issues confronting investment bankers. In particular, "Compliance" does not normally actively assist in identifying areas of future ethical problems.

Compliance and ethics, although related, are not synonymous. Compliance, as the name suggests, is about keeping to applicable rules and regulations. Ethics is about the underlying impact and intention of an action. It would, at least in theory, be possible to comply with rules in a way that is actively unethical (which is not to suggest that any compliance code is actually unethical). Although some branches of ethics are rules-based, the discipline is more often based on general principles, and the implementation of ethical principles can change over time.

The danger of compliance is that it is seen as the only necessary condition to carry out an activity, rather than as one of a number of conditions. Within an investment bank, in practice some investment bankers are likely to look down on compliance officers, and seek to get round any compliance regulation that might prevent them from making money from a transaction or an engagement.

There have been a series of compliance reviews and codes of practice for markets, quoted companies and banks. These have sometimes been knee-jerk responses to public and political concerns, and have not normally delivered significant changes in behaviour. For example, it is unclear whether the Sarbanes–Oxley regulations, introduced in the US in 2002 after the Enron and WorldCom collapses, caused a major improvement in corporate compliance so much as an increasing legal burden for company directors. Stephen Schwarzman, Chairman, Co-founder and CEO of the Blackstone Group, wrote in the *Wall Street Journal* (4 November 2008) that "Sarbanes-Oxley has made a fetish of compliance with complex regulations as a substitute for good judgment."[5]

Convergence of commercial and investment banking

The convergence of different areas of banking – notably commercial and investment banking – has given rise to both benefits and ethical problems. The argument by banks in favour of integration has been that it allows them to offer broader products to existing clients, products that those clients wish to purchase from their existing investment or commercial bank. In addition, it appears that an attempt to differentiate between investment banking and commercial banking can create relatively arbitrary distinctions.

Conversely, among the arguments for the separation of commercial and investment banking, advanced in the 1930s and again recently, is that it can prevent the domino effect of failing financial institutions that are each dependent on others' financial well-being, therefore reducing systemic risk. However, it is possible that an enforced split of commercial and investment banking could raise prices in certain markets, by reducing competition in some areas of activity.

The ethical analysis of the arguments for separating or not separating commercial and investment banking is complex. Essentially, it is to play off a reduction in the risk of catastrophic failure of the banking system – inevitably a rare event – against the benefit of allowing freedom of action and competition in the banking system. Ultimately, this is largely a political and regulatory but not an ethical question, provided (i) that a regulatory mechanism can be found that could prevent a significantly greater risk of banking failure if banks remain integrated and (ii) that it is possible to run an integrated (or universal) bank in an ethically consistent manner.

The fact that integrating investment banking and commercial banking products can give rise to ethical problems does not in itself make such a practice unethical, in the same way that while owning a shop or market stall and setting products out to be viewed by customers can give rise to the temptation to steal it is not tantamount to theft.

Too big to fail

The investment banking sector as a whole, and the largest players in the sector individually, are too big for Governments to allow them to fail. This implies that investment banks receive some form of economic free-ride.

There are different reasons why a company could be too big to fail: (a) the company itself is so important economically it could not be allowed to cease trading; (b) it provides essential services, and disruption to service supply could be unduly damaging for consumers; (c) its failure would spread to other companies, for example by creating a chain of defaults (such as via the non-payment of trade creditors); and (d) its failure would cause a systemic failure in a vital economic sector.

This presents a major ethical issue for Governments, but one that is not unique to investment banking. Governments face allowing a "free-ride" to investors, employees and other stakeholders in a range of enterprises that provide "essential" services or are of national "strategic" importance. Given the scale of banking failures, and the scale of finance provided to banks by Governments, this clearly applies to the banking sector – the failure of investment banks such as Lehman makes it less clear that this applies universally to investment banks. We would note that given the legal complexity around the failure of Lehman, it may be difficult to draw any specific lesson from the situation.

As stated above, "too big to fail" does not only affect investment banking. It affects a number of major industries, such as the car industry, which is seen as strategic in a number of countries (including France and the US) and the defence industry. It also applies, for other reasons, to the utility sector (gas, water and electricity), where its relevance is even greater than for the various areas of banking, due to the essential nature of the services provided. In the utility sector (commodity supplies such as electricity and water, which are generally natural monopolies), prices are regulated. In these sectors, it is sometimes argued that remuneration should be below levels for equivalent companies in other sectors, due to their protected nature. This type of protection extends to their revenue. A comparison cannot be drawn on the grounds of protected revenue or lack of competition between utilities and investment banking, where revenue is not protected and there are no natural monopoly characteristics.

The UK's Independent Commission on Banking stated that too big to fail "constitutes a perceived acceptance of risk by the state .... with the potential for the related rewards to be enjoyed by the private sector". This is described, in their Call for Evidence, as "inequitable" and "creating moral hazard incentives for poor decision making".[6]

Ethical duties and the implicit Government guarantee

The duty that investment banks owe to their Governments is affected by the implicit guarantee from Governments to support the financial markets. Investment banks have benefitted from this during the financial crisis – the liquidity crisis in the markets would have brought markets to some form of collapse without Government intervention.

The investment banking sector in general is still benefitting from Government intervention in markets, in the banking sector and in investment banking since 2008, which would increase the ethical duty owed by companies concerned. However, it can be argued that the increased ethical duty to Governments will at some stage reduce or even end, due to the steps taken by Governments to ensure that the investment banking and banking sectors (as well as the insurance sector) fund any future "rescue" in the sector. The implicit guarantee is now being reduced, to varying extents, in many countries through new legislation. It is also arguably offset at least in part by taxes paid by the investment banking sector.

Government intervention

Government intervention in the banking and investment banking sectors has had three main sources: first, intervention in financial markets;

second, direct funding of banks and investment banks, including acquiring or assuming toxic assets; and third, regulatory and legal reform. Government funding of investment banks (such as Goldman) or of commercial banks with major investment banking activities (such as RBS or Citi) has totalled hundreds of billions of dollars. In addition, some form of guarantee or toxic asset protection programme has also taken many hundreds of billions of dollars of risk away from bank (including investment bank) balance sheets.

At times during the financial crisis, even reducing interest rates to zero or near zero did not reduce the cost of borrowing in the way intended. LIBOR – the cost of money being loaned between banks – in normal market conditions trades closely in line with central bank base rates. During the financial crisis this gap widened dramatically, for example to 4–5 percentage points above base rates. LIBOR only reduced as Governments actively intervened to reduce rates through measures such as Quantitative Easing (QE). This involves a Government putting money into the banking system to increase reserves by buying financial instruments, typically Government bonds.

Governments have historically been in a position, when they wish, for example as an implied result of a democratic mandate, to determine how industrial and commercial sectors should operate. For a Government to find that in order to govern it is reliant on the financial stability of an unstable sector is politically problematic. It is debatable if Governments realised before 2007 that the financial sector is so large and so global that they do not control banks and investment banks in their jurisdictions, or even set interest rates entirely on their own (as the disconnect between LIBOR and base rates at times during the financial crisis demonstrated), nor are they able to control financial markets simply by regulation. This is both an economic and a political concern. It is also problematic that at least to some extent flawed regulatory structures or implementations were to blame for the financial crisis, alongside other issues including the sub-prime crisis, rating agency mistakes, and poor decisions at investment banks, commercial banks and investing institutions.

Lehman – Allowed to fail

It is important to note that investment banks have not all been "too big to fail". The highest profile investment bank to have failed was Lehman. In addition, there have been failures of smaller investment banks. Hedge funds have also been allowed to fail. In 1998, LTCM, a hedge fund, was bailed out by private investors rather than Government funding, in a rescue organised by the US Federal Reserve.

Events during the financial crisis tended not to happen in isolation. The bankruptcy of Lehman shows the impact of insolvency at a major investment bank, but was also part of the general crisis affecting the financial system. Lehman had substantial holdings in "toxic" real estate assets. In addition, Lehman provided liquidity to hedge funds, and the sudden withdrawal of liquidity had a major market impact.

Given that Lehman was allowed to fail, the extent of the free-ride in the investment banking sector as opposed to the banking sector and the implied increased ethical duty becomes less clear, although, as noted above, the legal situation regarding the failure of Lehman was complex, and it appears that the US Government may not have been legally able to prevent its failure. Nonetheless, the failure of some investment banks raises questions over the extent of implicit guarantees.

Insolvency and systemic risk

The failure of a company can take place in different ways, but would normally involve entering a bankruptcy proceeding. The impact of a sudden insolvency on an investment bank would be to tie up trading accounts and effectively freeze for an extended period the ability of counterparties to release cash. It would also undermine trading confidence and therefore undermine capital markets – without which the modern economy could not be sustained.

One lesson from the financial crisis is the extent to which the widespread use of derivatives to hedge some risks may in fact increase "systemic risk" – although this should not have been such a surprise, given that the experience of hedging risk is often not fully perfect and therefore frequently creates new or additional risks. It also became clear that the impact of the insolvency of a market participant can affect other participants that regulators cannot or are unlikely to know about. Market participants require capital to trade. Markets require liquidity, which would normally come from participants' capital. In extreme circumstances, this capital has to be augmented by public funds. The impact of a failure of one major market participant can be felt by a wide range of others: the sale of securities by counterparties or creditors needing to realise cash can cause a major fall in securities' prices.

Different jurisdictions have different laws and regulations relating to company insolvency. Notably, the US has chapter 11 of the Bankruptcy Code, which protects companies from creditors pending a court-approved reorganisation. The EU has no widely used direct equivalent, and each member state has its own insolvency regime. The relevant EU directive on insolvency relates to identifying the country of main interest, rather than applying a separate or overarching insolvency regime. EU member states typically regard trading while insolvent as a criminal act. The complexity of ownership and regulatory structures of investment banks, with activities domiciled in multiple jurisdictions with different insolvency regimes, makes the impact of a failure especially complex.

Legislative change

The legislative approaches to banking reform have varied greatly between countries. In the US, the Dodd–Frank Act (Dodd–Frank Wall Street Reform and Consumer Protection Act) has aimed to end the risk of "too big to fail" institutions being rescued by the state and has brought in major reforms aimed at providing financial stability, including a Financial Stability Oversight Council and Orderly Liquidation Authority. The Act stops short of requiring a separation of investment and commercial banking, which has been called for by some politicians.

The Dodd–Frank Act specifically aims to end "too big to fail" by a combination of measures, including regulation and supervision, a levy to be paid by major financial institutions to create an Orderly Liquidation Fund and provisions for orderly liquidation. The Act does not, however, set a limit on the size of financial institutions, including investment banks.

The Volcker Rule, also part of the Dodd–Frank Act (and named after its proponent, Paul Volcker, the former Chairman of the US Federal Reserve), restricts proprietary trading activities of banks (deposit-taking institutions), aimed at reducing risk-taking from deposit-taking. This rule has certain limitations, for example when determining hedging activities and when market-making. The likely impact of these limitations is currently unclear.

The UK's approach to legislative reform has been slower than in the US. On 16 June 2010, the UK Government announced the creation of the Independent Commission on Banking. The Commission has been asked to consider structural and related non-structural reforms to the UK banking sector to promote financial stability and competition. The Commission is due to report by the end of September 2011.

On 16 June 2010, the UK Government announced the formation of a new institution within the Bank of England, to be called the Financial Policy Committee (FPC), to manage risk within the financial system. The Treasury highlighted two potential sources of risk: first, systemic risk; and second, unsustainable levels of leverage, debt or credit growth. The FPC

will have powers over two new regulatory bodies, the Prudential Regulation Authority (PRA) and the Financial Conduct Authority (FCA). The FPC
will publish minutes of its deliberations and will be accountable to the
Treasury Select Committee.

Recent legislative change is aimed at reducing the wider impact
of failure of an investment bank or banks. It may also reduce the
risk of failure. It will not, however, deal with the other fundamental
issue of the competence of management and the behaviour of shareholders
of investment and commercial banks.

Ethical implications

The "too big to fail" argument has a number of ethical implications:

- "Too big to fail" can lead to an asymmetric risk–reward profile for
  investment bankers, encouraging relatively risky behaviour, which may
  be unethical with regard to both the investment bank's resources and
  potential Government liabilities.
- Pushing risk onto tax payers and away from shareholders and/or lenders
  can reduce the level of pay that is ethically acceptable within an
  investment bank, notably where the investment bank receives direct
  Government support.
- The profitability and stability of investment banking relies in part on
  Government support, which may impose an ethical duty on investment
  banks. To some extent this must have implicitly been the case prior to
  2007. However, such support in one form or another extends to most
  (if not all) sectors of the economy.
- A free-ride implies an increased ethical duty to support Government
  policy, potentially on a wide range of fronts, such as behaviour in the
  derivatives market or keeping to the spirit and not just the letter of tax
  codes.

Investment banks receive some form of "free-ride" by being able to rely
on various forms of Government protection. At the same time, like other
industrial sectors, investment banks are tax-paying, and therefore would
expect to benefit from some Government action.

The key question as to whether there is a real ethical concern relating
to a free-ride is whether the failure to regulate and understand credit risk
is "necessary" or inevitable, or whether it relates to a series of unfortunate
and specific failures. If the financial crisis is due, to a significant extent, on
regulatory failure, then the free-ride issue is less significant, with a lower

implied ethical duty to the Government. However, if the free-ride is of significant benefit under normal conditions, then the ethical duty to support the Government (e.g., by acting in ways to support Government policy in areas such as tax) is much greater.

Fiduciary duties

Directors of a company have legal duties to act in the interest of the company. These are "fiduciary" duties, which impose a high standard of behaviour. This extends to both executive and non-executive directors. There are differences in how this concept is applied in different jurisdictions. For example, in the UK, the Companies Act 2006 sets out directors' duties. In the US, the "Business Judgement Rule" is derived from case law. In practice, it is the responsibility of directors to act in the best interests of the company.

Under the UK's Companies Act 2006, directors have a duty to promote the success of the company. There is a (non-exhaustive) list of factors that directors have to take into account (section 172.1), including long-term consequences, interests of employees, relationships with suppliers and customers, the impact of decisions on community and environment, the desirability of maintaining a reputation for high standards of business conduct and the need to act fairly between members of the company. The UK Government provided guidance as to the meaning of "promoting the success" of a company. Lord Goldsmith stated at the Lords Grand Committee on 6 February 2006 that "For a commercial company, success will normally mean long term increase in value."[7]

Defining the long-term value of a company is not straightforward, especially for a large company with multiple businesses and assets. Value can be analysed using discounted cash flow analysis (DCF), although this has a number of subjective inputs, both in terms of methodology (e.g., discount rate) and in terms of business assumptions (e.g., market share), resulting in diverse outcomes. Value can also be assessed on the basis of comparisons with peers, where these are available, or on the basis of financial ratios, such as P:E (Price:Earnings) or multiples of enterprise value to EBITDA or cash flow (although multiple-based analysis tends to be cruder than DCF).

Shareholders

The ethics of the banking and investment banking sectors reflect prevailing business ethics. One of the major influences on publicly quoted companies is their shareholders. Shareholders can have a significant effect on the strategies of major companies. Institutional shareholders are primarily concerned with share price performance, and their influence is normally in the form of discussing companies' financial performances and strategies in the light of their financial results. The pressure from shareholders on quoted banks, notably on the universal banks, which combine the utility-type activities of commercial/retail banking with investment banking, may have had the effect of encouraging changing standards of behaviour in order to increase returns, for example by increasing the level of loans "sold" to retail customers, or increasing the level of capital committed to principal investment or trading strategies, each of which has possible ethical implications.

Shareholders rightly exercise influence over the companies they invest in, and on their boards. At times, shareholders can put pressure on company boards and executives to take increased risks. Shareholder support – or the lack of it – for companies has clearly affected the behaviour of some banks and investment banks, but such pressure is not always far-sighted. In 2007, there was extensive external pressure on HSBC to reform its activities, including pressure from activist shareholders. It became clear from late 2007 onwards, as the financial crisis developed, that while HSBC had eschewed some short-term opportunities for profits, despite high-profile exposure to sub-prime loans in the US, its shareholder value had been more effectively stewarded than that of many other UK and global banks.

Institutional shareholders have demanded high returns from commercial banking, potentially higher than could be sustained in the long term from a quasi-utility activity. Pressure from shareholders can effectively change a company's strategy. The pressure to lift commercial banking returns from utility-type levels (*c.* 10–12%) to investment banking levels (*c.* 20%) was applied both internally and externally within integrated banks and was one of the drivers of increased risk in the banking sector. Such returns were in part achievable from taking (principal) risk in investment banking. There is an interesting question as to the role of major institutional investors in creating the environment that led to the financial crisis. For shareholders, there is always pressure to seek performance from investee companies. Pressure is put on institutional investors by either trustees (in the case of pension or endowment funds) who have their own fiduciary duties or by retail investors seeking to maximise their returns by investing with the best-performing funds. Looking at the ethical behaviour of banks and investment banks in isolation of their shareholders, and their shareholders' stakeholders, will give only a limited picture of the basis of investment banks' behaviour.

Although there are fiduciary duties on shareholders to seek higher returns, these duties should not encourage shareholders to require investee companies to increase returns regardless of the impact on their risk profile, or prompt investee companies to behave unethically. It is the nature of shareholdings in quoted companies that they are more or less liquid. In which case, it is difficult for shareholders' incentives to always apply in the long term, given the scope to trade out of a holding (e.g., following periods of outperformance).

Voting

Shareholders do not have clear ethical duties regarding their normal involvement with companies in which they invest. Shareholders of quoted companies, including shareholders of investment banks, have the right to vote on resolutions proposed at a company's annual general meeting (AGM). This right can sometimes be regarded as an ethical "duty", requiring shareholders to actively participate in the governance of investments.

Shareholders have other mechanisms for exercising their rights or duties as shareholders. These include proposals of shareholder resolutions, more common in the US than Europe, and asking questions at company AGMs, but their real impact is limited. There are counterarguments that say that by appointing an appropriate board to manage a company, shareholders are exercising their responsibility adequately, and that it is not necessary to propose or support shareholder resolutions.

When considering whether to raise or support a shareholder resolution, the subject of the resolution is of primary importance. However, it is also important to consider whether a resolution is capable of being implemented. A badly drafted resolution may not be capable of proper implementation by a board. If a shareholder supports the spirit of a resolution, but believes the resolution is not capable of being implemented, there can be an ethical dilemma over whether the shareholder should support the resolution.

Although investment banks will frequently own significant (in monetary terms) holdings in companies' shares, where this is part of day-to-day trading and provision of liquidity to clients, it may not be practical to exercise voting rights on those shares. In other cases, where a holding may be part of a proprietary investment strategy, it is possible to exercise voting rights. Ethically, as a responsible shareholder, it would be expected that in such circumstances voting rights would be exercised.

Strategic issues – Success and competition

To be successful, investment banks need to be focused. An investment bank that compromises its business standards will not be as successful as others, and may risk some form of failure. By implication, compromising profit in order to support an ethical approach may appear to be a high-risk strategy. As can be seen from observing the length of time that "bubbles" can last in investment banking products, as well as the scale that they can reach, to avoid participating in markets as flawed but as large as the collatoralised debt obligations (CDO) market could prove costly for an investment bank, especially one independent of a commercial bank.

There are exceptions to this: there are niche markets for advisory firms where reputation is of especially great value, and therefore efforts to maintain reputational value become more important and the damage caused by a public ethical breach is greater. For some investment banks, reputation may be of paramount importance.

In general, the more an investment bank is dependent on its use of capital, the less it may need to fear damage to its reputation; whereas, the greater the reliance on client business, especially on advisory activities, the greater the need to protect its reputation for integrity.

This raises interesting questions about how reputational value is managed at integrated investment banks, which cover advisory activities as well as capital markets. In many cases, there is a tension between different activities, not just between different divisions but even between different trading or advisory teams in the same firm.

An investment bank's ability to hire and retain staff and provide acceptable returns to shareholders (either employees or external shareholders) depends both on absolute financial performance and on its competitive position in the market.

It is therefore significantly harder for an individual investment bank to adopt a self-denying approach to activities that may present ethical problems, such as trading activities in overvalued securities, if there is no industry-wide regulatory prohibition in place. The onus on an investment bank to behave ethically is unlikely to prove effective in the absence of some form of regulation. The effect of some investment banks behaving ethically in the context of a wider market not doing so may be the (possibly short-term) decline of the "ethical" investment banks, leaving a market dominated by less ethically minded participants.

Although the broad thrust of regulation in some jurisdictions is to separate investment banking and commercial banking, this may result in placing more pressure on investment banks to ignore ethical issues. The value and relatively stable income from a commercial bank may encourage shareholders and boards to support relatively ethical behaviour on the part of its investment banking activities. Empirical evidence does not, however, suggest that this is always the case – the investment banking arms of commercial banks were in some cases very involved in some of the abuses of the financial crisis.

In the long term, attention to ethical issues can prevent major problems – both financial and regulatory. In the short term, the incentive for investment bankers is to maximise revenue and profits. This incentive may also be shared by shareholders. Investment banking is a highly competitive industry. Without appropriate external regulation, investment banks may not be able to afford to be ethical. Purely prescriptive regulation – based on detailed rules – has major shortcomings, in part due to the speed of market innovation.

Ethical implications for investment banks

- The systemic issues raised by the financial crisis have an ethical dimension.
- There is nothing intrinsically unethical about investment banking or capital markets, but markets are not "moral-free zones".
- Investment banking is a necessary part of the modern economy, and fulfils a genuine market need, which can be seen as ethically beneficial.
- Ethical failings within the investment banking sector include greed and *hubris*.
- Investment banks have generally managed Compliance effectively. However, Compliance is not structured so as to spot future ethical concerns.
- Given that investment banking is a highly competitive industry, self-regulation is unlikely to bring about material change in ethical practices without an outside impetus.
- Investment banks have received some form of free-ride. The demise of Lehman raises the question of how great is the implicit guarantee given specifically to investment banking as opposed to the banking sector. Other sectors also benefit from a free-ride in this sense.
- The free-ride and the implicit Government guarantee impose an ethical duty on investment banks. This may be in part obviated by increased taxes and regulatory reform.
- Fiduciary duties impose legal obligations on directors of investment banks, effectively to maximise long-term value.

- Investment banks may not ethically be required to "believe" in the long-term value of securities or businesses they sell, but ethically they are required to be able to justify their valuation.
- The right to vote as a shareholder can also be an ethical duty.

Chapter summary

- A number of high-profile and highly damaging incidents have raised ethical concerns over finance.
- Investment banking performs functions necessary to support the modern economy. In terms of advisory and capital market activities, the investment banking sector has established itself and grown into a major global industry on the basis of fulfilling a market need for its services.
- Directors of a company have "fiduciary" duties to act in the interest of the company. These impose a high standard of behaviour.
- Banking is one of a number of industries that has an implicit Government guarantee and is "too big to fail". It is not clear to what extent this extends to all investment banks – Lehman was allowed to fail. The benefit of an implicit Government guarantee gives rise to increased ethical duties.
- Legislative change in some markets, aiming to end the implicit guarantee, may obviate at least some of the increased ethical duty.
- Shareholders rightly exercise influence over the companies in which they invest. For shareholders, there is always pressure to seek performance from investee companies.
- It is significantly harder for an individual investment bank to adopt a self-denying approach to activities that may present ethical problems, such as trading activities in overvalued securities, if there is no industry-wide regulatory prohibition in place.
- Although the broad thrust of regulation is to separate investment banking and commercial banking, this may result in more pressure being placed on investment banks to ignore ethical issues.

Do investment banks have a unique "implicit Government guarantee"? Does this, together with benefits resulting from Government support for the banking system during the financial crisis, impose specific ethical duties on investment banks?

3
Developing an Ethical Approach to Investment Banking

Examining the activities of investment banks from an ethical perspective involves looking not only in depth at the practices of investment banks and the underlying reasons for these practices (something that much of the recent critical commentary in the popular press fails to do) but also at the basis for ethical decision-making. This is a complex area, as there is no universal blueprint for thinking and acting ethically. There are various schools of thought, which highlight different ethical insights, all of which may have some relevance for investment banking.

What we will seek to do, therefore, is to draw on the main traditions of the moral philosophy that underpins business ethics to devise an ethical framework for investment banking. We acknowledge that there will be many areas of uncertainty, however, either because of disagreements as to what is ethical and unethical or most desirable, or because of lack of information on which to base decisions due to the imprecise nature of economic and financial forecasting. Nevertheless, such a framework provides a tool for applying ethical thought to decision-making.

The key point of business ethics is not so much to work out with clarity what is right or wrong in every situation, but to bring ethical criteria to bear where appropriate in business so that decisions are made that strive to be for the good because they are informed by ethical considerations.

An ethical framework for investment banking

Broadly speaking, moral philosophy has focused on three areas: (a) determining the moral rules and the duties we have towards each other that should govern our lives, (b) assessing the moral consequences of our actions and (c) developing the human characteristics that promote good behaviour. These have been worked out in three main schools of thought: deontological, consequentialist and virtue ethics.

Deontological ethics

Deontological ethics takes its name from *deos*, the Greek word for duty. This branch of moral philosophy is grounded in the understanding that there are universal moral principles or "duties" that should govern our behaviour. From this perspective, it is possible to discern moral absolutes – things that are clearly right or wrong – and ways of interacting with one another that are good. Deontological ethics therefore provide the ethical rules and values by which we should live. Obvious examples of moral absolutes are not to murder, torture or deliberately do harm, and examples of duties are to treat people fairly and with honesty.

Deontological ethics has its roots in the concept of natural law. The belief of there being a universal moral code that should be followed in order to lead a "good life" was central to the thinking of the Greek philosopher Aristotle (384–322 BCE), whose influence goes far beyond the ancient world, and also to the Christian theologian and philosopher Thomas Aquinas (1225–74). Natural law is grounded in both classical philosophy and a theological understanding that there is a moral code to the universe that has been divinely revealed and is accessible through human reason and thought. The Wisdom literature of the Jewish Scriptures (the Christian Old Testament) is an example of this, and it is expressed in the Christian tradition in Paul's Letter to the Romans, which speaks of what is required to live a godly life being "written on their hearts, to which their own conscience also bears witness" (Romans 2:15).

Natural law is not only the preserve of religions and classical philosophy, however. Philosophers coming from a secular Enlightenment perspective have also been drawn by the concept of there being common moral principles deeply ingrained within human nature. For John Locke (1632–1704), there are universal human rights, which should dictate our behaviour towards one another. Such a view has proved highly influential and shaped national and international law. Immanuel Kant (1724–1804) argued that our duties towards one another can be determined by human reason and without recourse to religion.

There is, for Kant, a "categorical imperative" that should determine behaviour. One of its formulations says "Act in such a way that you always treat humanity, whether in your own person or in the person of any other, never simply as a means, but always at the same time as an end." This imperative of having a duty to respect one another resonates with the "Golden Rule", an ancient ethical principle found in most religions and cultures: "Do to others as you would have them do to you." The widespread nature of the Golden Rule gives strong support to the concept of there being deeply ingrained moral principles shared across humanity.

In other formulations, Kant's categorical imperative states "Act only according to that maxim by which you can at the same time will that it should become a universal law" and "act only so that the will through its maxims could regard itself at the same time as universally lawgiving." Again, both of these point towards there being universally agreed and universally applicable ethical principles. The acid test in terms of determining whether our behaviour is right or wrong is whether, if everyone did the same, the overall outcome would be good or bad. For instance, if everyone persistently lied, truth and trust would be undermined, and these are fundamental to the good ordering of society. Lying is therefore immoral.

Another important aspect of deontological ethics is justice: treating people fairly so that in any given situation everyone gets what society deems they deserve. Economics and business raise a number of issues of justice primarily related to distribution. For instance, it is often argued that markets are "just" or "fair" in that they determine, through the interacting forces of supply and demand, the prices of goods and services and their allocation in a way that takes into account the various needs of consumers and producers. However, not all ethical questions of distribution are dealt with by the "invisible hand" of the market, to use Adam Smith's famous term. As was discussed earlier, for reasons of equity some market participants may need protection from adverse market forces.

An influential contemporary theory of justice, which has been applied to economics, is that developed by the philosopher John Rawls. Rawls' theory of justice centres on two principles, which can be used to determine whether or not an action is just. Rawls' first principle of justice is that each person is to have an equal right to the most extensive scheme of equal basic liberties compatible with a similar scheme of liberties for others. Rawls' second principle is that inequalities should be arranged such that (i) they are to be of the greatest benefit to the least-advantaged members of society, and (ii) that there is equality of opportunity in terms of employment.

The first principle focuses on universal human rights to ensure that basic freedoms are available to everyone affected by a decision. The second acknowledges that inequalities are inevitable in a society that is free and where there is competition. However, for reasons of equity (rather than equality) an economic or business decision is just (i) only if those who benefit least from it are still better off than they would be had that decision not been taken, and (ii) only if there is equality of opportunity in terms of employment (so that, in theory at least, all could gain the maximum benefit).

As will be seen later, Rawls' theory of justice is particularly useful with regard to the ethics of remuneration in investment banking.

Consequentialist ethics

In contrast, the consequentialist approach to ethics focuses on outcomes rather than moral absolutes. The basic principle of this form of ethical thinking is that it is paramount to assess what would be the best or the most desirable result when making a decision.

An influential consequentialist thinker was Thomas Hobbes (1588–1679), who argued that humans are fundamentally self-interested and should act in ways that maximise their own long-term interests. Similarly, Adam Smith (1723–90) argued that the pursuit of individual self-interest was permissible because it produced a morally desirable outcome through the workings of the "invisible hand" of the market. However, the best-known and most influential form of consequentialist ethics is utilitarianism, the underlying principle of which is that we should act in such a way that maximises the good, happiness, pleasure or "utility" of the greatest number of people. Associated in particular with the work of Jeremy Bentham (1748–1832) and John Stuart Mill (1806–73), utilitarianism has provided the philosophical underpinning of much economic theory, where utility maximisation is a key guiding principle, and applied economics. Perhaps one reason for this is that utilitarianism lends itself to quantification, enabling ethical criteria to be applied in cost–benefit analysis. An important – and controversial – example of this is the use of the "quality-adjusted life year" (QALY) in health economics. A QALY is an arithmetical measure that seeks to take into account the quality and quantity of a patient's life, and is used to make (often hard) decisions about resource allocation in health care.

Although influential and clearly of ethical relevance, utilitarianism has proved controversial. There is no consensus as to how utility is defined and measured, for instance. Nor, in many cases, is it clear what the likely consequences of taking a decision will be. Unpredictability is a fact of life. There may also be multiple consequences to consider – both positive and negative – that create the problem of how to weigh up the pros and cons of a decision. The assertion that outcomes, however desirable they might be, should take priority over other ethical considerations has also been widely questioned.

Despite the criticisms levelled at utilitarianism, consequentialist ethics remains an important, if incomplete, branch of moral philosophy, and rightly so because assessing possible outcomes should be part of the moral compass when making decisions. This too is in harmony with the natural law approach to ethics in which there is an inherent understanding that we should act so as to maximise that which is good.

Virtue ethics

A third influential area of moral philosophy (which is becoming increasingly influential in a business context) is virtue ethics. This also has its roots in classical thought, especially the work of the Greek philosopher Plato (428/427–348/347 BCE), and was developed further in the Middle Ages by Aquinas. The thrust of virtue ethics is that there are desirable human traits or characteristics that naturally work to promote that which is good – "the Disposition to act well", to quote Aquinas. The main or "cardinal" or "natural" virtues that achieve this are: courage, temperance, prudence and justice. By temperance, what is meant is that our behaviour should be governed by reason rather than emotional drives and instinct, and likewise prudence means having the capacity to make wise judgements on ethical matters.

Whereas deontological and consequentialist ethics focus on what we should do and how we know what we should do, virtue ethics is about what sort of persons we should be, because our behaviour is heavily dependent upon our character. Virtuous behaviour cannot be seen in isolation from ethical behaviour because it is by acting ethically over and over again that virtuous habits are developed, and it is by developing virtuous characteristics that we are more likely to act ethically – the two are inextricably linked and interact.

An interesting and important question is whether there are particular behavioural characteristics associated with investment banking that, at first sight, may seem unethical, but are in reality virtuous. The answer is probably yes – and it hinges on whether the behaviour is associated with pursuing what is good. For instance, given that the industry is competitive and market-driven, it can be argued that achieving the best deal is highly desirable in terms of ensuring that the fairest price is determined. Achieving this may involve aggressive and apparently ruthless behaviour. If the motive behind the behaviour is to achieve the best price, then it can be virtuous – but if the motive is to hurt another in the deal, then the virtue becomes a vice. A parallel can be drawn in a court of law. Aggressive questioning by a barrister that is designed to determine the truth is virtuous as it serves the pursuit of justice, whereas aggressive questioning motivated by the desire to demean, humiliate or frighten is morally unacceptable. In short, virtuous behaviour is not the same as being nice or friendly.

Ethical behaviour

In practice, the moral decisions that we make – what we deem right or wrong, good or bad, desirable or undesirable – are rarely made with precision or logic within the framework of a particular school of thought. Instead, moral consciousness is shaped by a mixture of experience, views, convictions, beliefs and personality traits, and how much weight we might place on any of these might depend on circumstances.

The complexity of moral reasoning is something explored by the contemporary philosopher Alasdair MacIntyre. MacIntyre is critical of the way that ethical reflection is often conducted, leading to ill-thought-through decisions. A particular concern is "moral relativism" – regarding ethics as essentially a product of culture rather than being universally grounded.[1] The temptation of such an outlook is to draw upon various ethical criteria to rationalise what we *want* to do, rather than to work out from a reasoned ethical framework what we *ought* to do. We share this concern.

There is clearly great value in the three approaches to ethics outlined above. In our (non-relativistic) view, there are clear moral principles that should be followed in all walks of life – banking being no exception. However, there may be situations in business where moral absolutes are insufficient to identify what to do. When this is the case, the likely ethical consequences of a business decision can complement them. In general, ethical decision-making involves the sort of moral reasoning that the virtuous characteristics described above encourage.

What is clear is that deontological, consequentialist and virtue ethics can and do interrelate. A good example of this is the "just war" approach to conflict, which for centuries has been used to determine whether or not going to war is morally acceptable. This approach requires meeting a range of ethical criteria: first, the cause for which armed combat is proposed must be regarded as just from a deontological point of view, such that it should protect civilians from infringements of their human rights; second, from the perspective of virtue ethics, action should be taken for the right motives – compassion for fellow human beings rather than, say, to further political or economic power; and third, the likely consequences of the action should be assessed, and if the likely costs (such as civilian deaths) outweigh the benefits of taking the action, then it is ethical not to proceed.

Bearing this in mind, a logical way to put the theory of ethics into practice in a business context is to work within a framework informed by consequentialist, deontological and virtue ethics. This avoids the trap of moral relativism, but acknowledges the contribution each approach to ethics has to offer to help us behave in such a way as to maximise the good consequences of what we do within the bounds of what we believe our moral responsibilities to be.

A practical way of thinking ethically is to consider the following questions when making a decision:

1. What values are relevant in the situation, and what bearing will they have in making a decision?
2. What rights are relevant in the situation, and what bearing will they have in making a decision?
3. Who are the stakeholders, and what duties are they owed?
4. What are the likely intended or unintended consequences of taking a decision?
5. What virtues will be developed or compromised by acting in a particular way?

This approach does not necessarily mean that those facing the same issue will come up with the same answer. Take an example from a different area of finance: giving development aid to a country governed by a dictatorship. Operating in such a political climate, one aid agency may take a pragmatic, consequentialist approach and decide not to challenge the dictator but rather continue to deliver services to the people to ensure they continue to receive aid to maximise their immediate material well-being. Another agency working in the same country may take a more deontological approach and publicly challenge violations to human rights, thereby running the risk of being forced out of the country and bringing their aid to a halt. Both are arguably acting ethically – and indeed in this case their different conclusions, each reached on ethical grounds, may complement one another.

Moral reasoning and investment banking

This brings us to the point where we can begin to identify some key principles for constructing an ethical framework for investment banking. At this stage it is worth reminding ourselves of the main functions of investment banks, as all ethical criteria must relate to these. We regard investment banks as having four main functions, all of which have the potential to serve good ends. The purpose of ethics is to ensure that they do. These functions are: (a) to raise capital required for investment, (b) to provide liquidity for markets to function effectively, (c) to provide a wide range of beneficial financial services to the public and private sectors, and (d) to create financial instruments designed to meet market needs.

How, then, do these functions relate to the ethics discussed in this chapter?

Deontological ethics – Trust

It is widely recognised that for financial markets to function and for banks to operate effectively there must be a high level of trust. Investors must have the confidence to entrust their money to others in order to provide the necessary capital for investment, otherwise the system collapses.

Trust is engendered by confidence, and in business confidence is engendered by two things: (a) competence – a belief that a firm has expertise and knows what it is doing, and (b) the trustworthiness of its management and employees. In this respect, technical and ethical considerations go hand in hand. Firm A may have high levels of technical expertise, but poor ethical standards. Firm B may have scrupulous ethical standards but poor technical expertise. Both firms, A and B, run the risk of loss of confidence and trust for very different reasons. A "good" firm must be both technically competent and morally trustworthy.

A business that develops a culture where values such as fairness, honesty and integrity are encouraged and rewarded will build up trust with those with whom it engages. So, too, will a firm that recognises its duties to stakeholders – particularly its investors, employees, clients and society at large. Also, from a deontological perspective, a firm that does not circumvent the law, or the regulatory framework within which its industry operates, is more likely to be trusted.

The trust required to facilitate the efficient operation of markets is very specific and is not a general trust in the different participants in a market. Market operation relies on trust that participants will settle their trades (pay when required and deliver the securities bought) and financially can stand behind their trading positions. While being trustworthy is an example of virtuous behaviour, the type of trust on its own required to enable market operations does not make market participants or markets specifically virtuous or ethical. The major ethical feature of markets is their delivery of efficient – or fair – prices for both buyers and sellers. **Trust in markets has very specific and limited ethical qualities.**

Investment banks take issues of trust very seriously. However, there are also great temptations to abuse the trust of clients, from the perspective of both advisory business and the capital markets. In their advisory businesses, the top few investment banks relentlessly target an advisory role in every major transaction, and the top investment banks continue to be represented in most very large transactions. Given the relatively small number of global companies capable of participating in $10 billion+ deals, this means that the investment banks continue to be trusted and/or required by major corporations. Most investment banks manage relationships with major corporations on an integrated basis: banking and investment banking services can be supplied through a single relationship manager or team. Therefore, accessing business in capital markets relies on retaining a position of trust. Investment banking league tables suggest that the established major investment banks retain their positions as the leading advisers to major corporations because they have a relationship that is based at least in part on trust.

An investment bank can be retained for its services for a number or combination of reasons. It is not the case that an investment bank is hired to advise a client on the basis purely of its trustworthiness. The investment bank could also be hired for its ability to execute a transaction (get things done), requiring less a trusted adviser and more a mercenary one – willing to execute a mandate in exchange for a fee. It would be a mistake to assume that all investment banks market themselves in the same way, or that all clients look for the same qualities. Many highly capable investment bankers are able to adopt different approaches to managing relationships with different clients. For an investment bank with a good relationship with an established client, the knowledge that the investment bank had had a high-profile ethical problem would probably not on its own prejudice the ongoing relationship (unless the ethical problem was very extreme). However, bad publicity on ethics would be likely to deter a new client from retaining the investment bank.

The trust required for markets to operate is trust that trades will be executed and settled. While this is ethical, it is at the same time very limited. Markets – and investment banks, or traders – do not require other forms of trust in order for participants to be able to make money from market trading. Trust is more important for advisers (such as in M&A) than for trading. Although advisory services rely on technical skills and forms of intellectual property as well as trust, their business could be severely affected if they were generally untrustworthy.

Deontological ethics – Stakeholders

During the financial crisis, questions were raised about banks' duties to stakeholders. For instance, amid the controversy over bonuses, one important point raised was that bank employees often appear to receive a disproportionate share of profits compared with the banks' shareholders (notably in the investment banking arms of commercial banks), and this was seen by some as inequitable. Questions were also raised about investment banks' attitudes to clients.

Some investment banks' high-risk operations, which contributed to causing a recession, also raised questions about the banks' duties to society at large and their apparent lack of awareness of wider responsibilities. In a letter sent from the learned society, the British Academy, to Queen Elizabeth II in response to her question, "why had nobody noticed that the credit crunch was on its way?" its authors, Professors Tim Besley and Peter Hennessy, describe "a failure of the collective imagination of many bright people, both in this country and internationally, to understand the risks to the [economic] system as a whole".[2]

The financial crisis also raised fundamental questions about the creation of complex financial instruments that contributed to market instability. While, on the one hand, these instruments, such as CDOs, are designed to provide investment opportunities to help smooth out long-term market volatility, some are also designed to circumvent regulatory control, and ended up exacerbating the market volatility they were supposed to dampen.

The financial crisis therefore highlighted a number of significant issues in which duties to others and the pursuit of the good came into question.

Another area where investment banks have long come in for criticism concerns human rights. While at first sight it may appear that human rights – the right of free speech, worship and assembly, the right to life, food, clothing, shelter and so on – have little to do with investment banks, this is not the case. The nature of the clients a bank does business with, and the projects it supports through investment, may well raise serious issues of human rights. An investment bank that sources capital for a corrupt government or investment for weapons manufacture or projects that impact on the well-being of communities will inevitably – and rightly – come under scrutiny for its ethical stance.

Other rights are also important. Employment rights are as relevant to investment banking as elsewhere, and so too are intellectual property rights, as will be seen in Chapter 5.

Consequentialist ethics

Another area of concern heightened by the financial crisis relates to consequentialist ethics. On 14 September 2007, the UK government decided to bail out the failing retail bank Northern Rock, which came under state ownership. The UK Government decided that the negative consequences of allowing this bank to collapse were too great for society to bear, and so it decided to take over the bank to protect the investments of individuals and institutions. Exactly one year later, the US government took the opposite decision with regard to the investment bank Lehman, although it had previously come to the aid of the failing Federal National Mortgage Association and Federal Home Loan Mortgage Corporation (Fannie Mae and Freddie Mac). In the case of Lehman, as well as arguments regarding the legal ability to carry out a rescue, the negative consequences of a bailout to the US economy were seen as outweighing the benefit of preventing the firm's collapse.

Within the firms themselves, decisions had been taken which clearly had not anticipated the consequences that transpired. The uncertainty of financial markets and of economic forecasting poses a problem for investment bankers and all involved in financial services, as well as for economic policymakers.

From an ethical perspective, while possible consequences to investment banking decisions must always be taken into account, we believe that given the risks associated with the high degree of uncertainty, it is ethically irresponsible to place too much emphasis on possible consequences. In the face of uncertainty in the markets, decision-making that is based on reason, and awareness of duties to stakeholders (notably clients, but also shareholders) are paramount. It could be argued that this has not been the case in banking in recent times, and was a contributory factor to the financial crisis.

Virtue ethics

Economics, more than any other discipline, has considered how to incentivise different behaviours, but has rarely considered whether those behaviours are virtuous. Writing about the emergence of "casino capitalism" in the 1980s, Susan Strange, a professor at the London School of Economics, commented that when luck takes over from skill and hard work, "Respect for ethical values…suffers a dangerous decline."[3] A concern – from the outside at least – is that the speculative nature of the trading that is a core part of investment banking can indeed erode values.

While the suggestion that traders engage in reckless gambling is a gross distortion of the skill of those working within a (speculative) market, it nevertheless highlights the importance of ethics within investment banking, and the importance of encouraging virtuous behaviour.

In the 1990s, the activities of Nick Leeson highlighted the significance of personal character in investment banking. More recently, the case of Jérôme Kerviel provides a stark reminder of the dangers of reckless behaviour. Kerviel placed bets within the markets worth more than the entire capital of his firm, the French bank Société Générale, for which he received a five-year prison sentence and was fined €4.9 billion – the amount lost by Société Générale in January 2008 because of his rogue trading.

This case highlights the importance of ethics in investment banking, and the need for an integrated approach. The integrity of the industry depends on the character of its decision-makers (virtue ethics). However, the fact that individuals were allowed to go unchecked raises questions not only of management, but also of regulation (deontological ethics). The impact on Société Générale and the wider economy makes clear, as well, the importance of assessing risks and outcomes (consequentialist ethics).

Codes of Ethics

Many investment banks have attempted to provide some sort of ethical framework in which to operate, in the form of "Codes of Ethics". **If an investment bank is serious about ethics, generating a useful code to guide employees is an important step. Inculcating its use is significantly harder, but it can form an essential protection of shareholder value. While the general approach of existing Codes, based on general principles rather than detailed rules, may have some advantages over the prescriptive approach taken by some regulatory bodies, given the rate of innovation and development in investment banking, existing Codes of Ethics have limited practical use and are generally disappointing. Investment banks that promulgate "ethical" behaviour fail to define its meaning, or educate employees as to its practice.**

Despite our misgivings about existing Codes, we believe that Codes of Ethics should form a useful starting point for any consideration of ethics in investment banking. However, the Codes are generally both vague and self-serving (at least as focused on protecting shareholders as clients), and, as such, in practical terms offer little assistance in assessing ethical dilemmas faced by investment bankers.

However, Codes of Ethics also have an attribute that is generally positive: they are based on broad ethical principles. This overall approach can be helpful in providing ethical guidance, if it is sufficiently clear what the principles mean in practice.

We have reviewed some of the major investment banks' Codes of Ethics and/or Conduct, although the summary presented here is not exhaustive, given the similarity of many of these Codes. In general, they provide insubstantial ethical guidance on how to treat clients, and are more concerned with protecting the firm and shareholders from abuse by employees. One legitimate reason for the vague nature of these Codes is the disparate nature of the roles carried out, especially in an integrated investment bank.

We have focused initially on the Goldman Sachs' Code of Business Conduct and Ethics, as it has been recently reviewed by Goldman, and the review itself as well as the changes in the Code are instructive. Goldman Sachs has reviewed its business standards and Code of Ethics in the light of the financial crisis. In the previous Code of Business Conduct and Ethics (as of 2009),[4] a significant proportion of the Code related to protecting the firm or its shareholders from abuse by the employee – for example, by failing to protect confidential information. The Code quoted Goldman's Business Principles and states that "Integrity and honesty are at the heart of our business." The Code only dealt with day-to-day questions relating to business ethics in one section out of nine in total, a section on "Fair Dealing". This section was very broad and notably includes the sentence, "We do not seek competitive advantages through illegal or unethical business practices." The Goldman Sachs ethical policy as far as clients was concerned therefore appeared to be based on the concept of "fair dealing". In the US, "fair dealing" is also a legal concept associated with full disclosure. It is therefore unclear what meaning the various Codes of Ethics are applying to the phrase.

The sections covered in this Code are:

Compliance and Reporting
Personal Conflicts of Interest
Public Disclosure
Compliance with Laws, Rules and Regulations
Corporate Opportunities
Confidentiality
Fair Dealing
Equal Employment Opportunity and Harassment
Protection and Proper Use of Firm Assets
Waivers of This Code

The Goldman Code of Business Conduct and Ethics and the Goldman Business Principles did not provide the basis for detailed discussion of

Goldman's role in ABACUS by the Senate Permanent Subcommittee on Investigations, reinforcing the impression that it is of marginal importance in practical ethical issues.

Goldman Sachs Business Principles

In January 2011, Goldman Sachs published a "Business Standards Report", which included its 14 Business Principles.[5] Goldman also updated its Code of Business Conduct and Ethics, which now directly refers to its Business Principles.

These principles start with a commitment to serving clients, and always putting clients first. They state a commitment to complying with both "the letter and spirit of the laws, rules and ethical principles that govern us". They also state that they expect employees to "maintain high ethical standards in everything they do". Although this refers to "ethical princi-ples" and "high ethical standards", the basis for making ethical decisions (as opposed to legal or rule-based) remains undefined.

The Business Standards Report makes a number of statements relating to ethics, either implicitly or explicitly:

- It states that the Business Principles were drawn up "30 years ago" and remain relevant today. It states, however, that the Code of Business Conduct and Ethics will be updated.
- The firm will put clients first and explain how different categories of client are treated.
- Employees will be required to "certify their compliance" to the Code of Business Conduct and Ethics. This latter requirement appears to be a reasonable attempt to make employees think about ethics – but is unlikely to be effective without real management intent to foster an ethical culture.
- It refers to "culture" and "values" forming part of compensation deci-sions. Although ethics are not explicitly mentioned here, they may be implied.
- It states that Goldman will consider whether it "should" rather than "could" engage in market activities relating to structured products.
- It states that values and culture will be considered as part of "recog-nition", including both promotion and compensation, suggesting that an employee's adherence to the firm's values will form a part of deci-sions on pay and promotion. It is unclear exactly to what extent such issues will affect decisions compared with more business-focused considerations.

Revised Code

The revised Code of Business Conduct and Ethics[6] also refers to the Business Principles. In a foreword, Goldman Chairman and CEO Lloyd Blankfein states that "It has often been said that one person can cause more harm to Goldman Sachs from a single bad decision than good to the firm over the course of a career." Despite the revisions, the Code does not explain how to assess "ethical standards". Conflicts of interest are covered in general terms. The body of the Code mentions conflicts of interest in the context of "personal conflicts of interest". The "Preamble" states that "if a transaction generates a conflict that cannot be addressed, we would prefer to lose the business than to abandon our principles". The Code refers also to a Compendium, available on the firm's internal website, containing additional detailed policies and procedures.

Other investment banking Codes of Ethics

Given the similarity between many of the Codes of Ethics, we have taken only two further Codes, to assess what they tell employees about ethics, and how useful they are in practice. The Morgan Stanley Code of Ethics and Business Conduct[7] is similar to the previous Goldman Code. However, it deals specifically with conflicts of interest and also covers other areas, such as accepting gifts. Its opening section exhorts employees to "lead with integrity, put clients first, win in the marketplace, think like an owner, and keep your balance".

The Nomura Group Code of Ethics[8] states an additional principle. Whereas both Goldman Sachs and Morgan Stanley refer to dealing with clients in a "fair" manner, Nomura refers to acting fairly, but also to acting in the best interests of customers.

Increasingly, investment bankers are required to certify periodically that they have read and complied with their Code of Ethics. In the absence of this, it is doubtful how often employees in an investment bank refer to their employer's Code of Ethics. This assists in ensuring that the investment bank is perceived by employees to wish to have an ethical culture. Even where compliance with Codes is certified, it is doubtful that the codes as they currently exist are much practical use. In reality, the overwhelming day-to-day pressure on investment bankers is to complete profitable transactions or trades and secure revenue (and profit). A successful investment banker will typically be very focused on developing and completing a transaction or trade or developing a client relationship, and is unlikely to dwell on ethical issues, unless these issues are firmly inculcated in each department within an investment bank.

As stated below it is noteworthy that ethical investment groups, notably those connected with major faith groups, have specific policies aimed at sector-related concerns, but that investment banking Codes of Ethics do not even discuss such concerns. Investment banks will generally (but not always) take the view that they will not discriminate between legally permissible areas of economic activity.

The asymmetric risk-reward trade-off for an individual investment banker will inevitably put bankers in a position where they will have significant incentives to take major risks, including on ethical issues, which may not be in the interests of the overall investment bank. This ultimately is a management issue, but one that is not straightforward to resolve. Management and resolution of problems in this area require complex management of capital risk. Investment banks have established procedures in place to manage such risk, which in most circumstances are effective.

In other sectors with the risk of ethical problems, companies require employees to at least annually certify that they have complied with the relevant Code of Ethics. In a few cases, such certification is quarterly. This process keeps the Code of Ethics more clearly in employees' minds. Codes of Ethics in such sectors can be significantly more informative and helpful than those found in the investment banking sector. The US manufacturer and service provider Caterpillar has a 36-page "Code of Conduct" (some of which is glossy packaging), which includes a toll-free confidential helpline for employees. The UK company BAE Systems has a 63-page "Code of Conduct", which is available in five languages (the company cites six languages, but two of these are "US English" and "UK English"). This also guides employees to an "Ethics Helpline". These Codes provide significantly greater guidance to employees than that found in investment banking Codes in relation to day-to-day ethical issues.

Investment banking is necessary to support the modern economy. Capital markets have some intrinsic ethical qualities – but these are limited. The problems of the financial crisis are not unique, even in recent history. Regulation based on prescriptive rules has inherent failings, due to the speed of innovation in investment banking. Without regulatory constraints, investment banks are unlikely to be individually able to avoid unethical activities if such activities are highly profitable and legal. Separation of commercial and investment banking may offer protections to society, but it is difficult to see how separation would also necessarily increase incentives to prioritise ethics over profits. Investment bank Codes of Ethics have limited practical use and are generally disappointing. Investment banks that

promulgate "ethical" behaviour fail to educate employees as to the meaning of "ethical".

Ethical implications for investment banks

- Moral philosophy has three areas of focus, each of which are relevant to investment banking: rights and duties, consequences and virtuous behaviour, which together can form a framework for investment banking ethics. Caution should be applied to "moral relativism" – regarding ethics as a product of culture rather than being universally grounded – as this can lead to justifications for whatever we want to do.
- Banks have a duty to stakeholders, including shareholders and clients, and also to Government.
- Ethics and competence can be related.
- There is a concern that the speculative nature of trading by investment banks can erode values.
- Existing investment banking Codes of Ethics have limited value and need to be revised (see Chapter 9), although they have a positive attribute in being focused on broad principles.
- Ethical investors and faith groups have detailed policies regarding doing business with or investing in ethically contentious sectors. These are not considered in investment banking Codes of Ethics.
- Employees should regularly review and refer to their Code of Ethics.

Chapter summary

- There is no universal blueprint for thinking and acting ethically.
- The key point of business ethics is not so much to work out with clarity what is right in every situation, but to bring ethical criteria to bear where appropriate in business.
- The main traditions of the moral philosophy that underpins business ethics can be used to devise an ethical framework for investment banking.
- Moral philosophy has focused on three areas: (a) determining moral rules and duties, (b) assessing moral consequences and (c) developing the human characteristics that promote good behaviour.
- Deontological ethics is grounded in the understanding that there are universal moral principles or "duties" that should govern our behaviour.
- Consequentialist and utilitarian ethics focuses on outcomes rather than moral absolutes. The basic principle of this form of ethical thinking is what would be the best or most desirable result when making a decision.

- Virtue ethics is based on the idea that there are desirable human traits or characteristics that naturally work to promote that which is good.
- Whereas deontological and consequentialist ethics focus on what we should do and how we know what we should do, virtue ethics is about what sort of persons we should be, because our behaviour is heavily dependent upon our character.
- The moral decisions that we make are rarely done with precision or logic within the framework of a particular school of thought. Instead, moral consciousness is shaped by a mixture of experience, views, convictions, beliefs and personality traits, and how much weight we might place on any of these might depend on circumstances.
- A "good" firm must be both technically competent and morally trustworthy.
- The trust required for markets to operate is trust that trades will be executed and settled. While this is ethical, it is at the same time very limited.
- In the face of uncertainty in the markets, decision-making that is based on reason, and awareness of duties to stakeholders, is paramount. It could be argued that this has not been the case in banking in recent times, and was thus a contributory factor to the financial crisis.
- The integrity of the industry depends on the character of its decision-makers (virtue ethics).
- Existing investment bank Codes of Ethics have limited practical use and are generally disappointing. Notably, they do not define "ethical behaviour" or explain how to deal ethically with the predominant areas of ethical concern, including duty of care to clients and conflicts of interest.

What should be the focus of a Code of Ethics? Is this primarily a document to protect shareholders or clients, and is there a conflict between the interests of the two groups?

4
Religion and Business Ethics

Religions have long-standing approaches to ethics, including business ethics. Given the widespread influence of religion, this has helped shaped economic life over the centuries. Religious ethics form a major part of broader understandings of ethical issues. Many religions and denominations apply both an ethical screen to investment and also advocate specific ethical approaches to business. Both of these approaches can be relevant to investment banking. There are religious ethical objections to economic activity involving industrial sectors that are harmful, notably alcohol, tobacco, defence, gambling and pornography. Concerns over these sectors are shared by the world's major religions, including Christianity, Islam, Judaism, Hinduism and Buddhism. The three Abrahamic faiths in particular have significant commonality on ethical concerns regarding business issues including with regard to specific business sectors. However, there is a lack of consistency even among faith groups in how to address such issues in practice, indicating that it may not be straightforward for investment banks to reach clear policies themselves on a sector basis.

There are differences between religions and between denominations in their approach to ethical investment, and also between countries. The 3iG FCI Practitioners' Report[1] found that US-based faith-consistent investors placed relatively more importance on diversity and inclusion, and that non-US investors placed relatively more importance on transparency.

The past quarter of a century has seen the emergence of ethical concerns among investors and at company boards, in the form of ethical or socially responsible investment (SRI) among investors and SRI or CSR committees of company boards. Religious organisations have played a leading role in promoting this trend. There are also a number of large and well-established faith-based investors who manage their own funds on ethical principles. These tend to be Christian – which reflects a difference in establishment and history, as a number of large historical Christian denominations have central funds, whereas other religions tend to have less clear organisational structures. There is also a possible theological reason for the high level of Christian scrutiny paid to business ethics, notably ethical investment, as the teachings of Jesus found in the New Testament are particularly critical of how wealth is handled.

Below, we have set out a short summary of the approach of five major religions to business ethics, and have looked specifically at sector-based investment issues, an area of significant concern from the perspective of religious ethics, but almost entirely absent from the ethical thinking of investment banks. A specific analysis of sector-specific investment policies of the major faiths is of potential benefit to investment banks. Given the number of people professing these faiths in the Americas, Europe, the Middle East and Africa, arguably such policies could provide a guide as to economic involvement that would be ethically unacceptable to many cultures, even if not illegal. As investment banking activities have become the object of closer scrutiny, involvement in sectors that are ethically proscribed due to the harm they cause could become an area of scrutiny and concern. This issue should at least be considered by investment banks.

Christianity

Investment funds based on Christian principles tend to avoid (or ban) investments in a number of sectors, which are proscribed either for theological reasons, or for the harm caused to people and society. These sectors are typically: alcohol, tobacco, defence, gambling and pornography.

A number of faith leaders have also made specific statements or published more detailed analyses of the financial crisis.

Roman Catholic Church

On 29 January 2009, Pope Benedict XVI, the leader of the Roman Catholic Church, issued an "Encyclical", or official papal letter, called *Caritas in Veritate* (or *Love in Truth*).[2] This sets out key principles for markets and for managing businesses and the role of business in the context of the Catholic faith. It includes specific statements that "the economy needs ethics in order to function correctly" (para. 45) and that "Every economic decision has a moral consequence" (para. 37).

Paragraph 35 of the encyclical states that the market cannot work properly without "internal forms of solidarity and trust" – it needs "social cohesion" to work effectively. The encyclical describes this in terms of requiring not just commutative justice, which enables counterparties to agree a transaction, but also distributive justice and social justice, because a market cannot be independent of the wider society in which it works.

In paragraph 36, the encyclical gets close to describing markets as implicitly ethical, by stating that economic activities (including, implicitly, investment banking) are neither ethically neutral nor opposed to society. However, because markets are human, they "must be structured and governed in an ethical manner".

The idea that a corporation ought to be responsible to more than its shareholders, and that ethics are an intrinsic part of business decisions, is not novel, but is given new moral force within the Roman Catholic Church through this encyclical.

The Anglican Communion

Rowan Williams, the Archbishop of Canterbury and symbolic head of the Anglican Communion, said in a speech at Trinity Church on Wall Street in 2010 that economic activity "is subject to the same moral considerations as all other activities". In *Crisis and Recovery*[3] he argues that treating economic exchange as the only real type of human activity is akin to looking at life as purely a question of evolutionary biology, a question of competition and survival.

Within the Anglican Communion, the Church of England has a general statement on the ethics of its own investments of about £5 billion, issued by its Ethical Investment Advisory Group (EIAG), in its "Statement of Ethical Investment Policy".[4] This specifically covers the Church's own investments, rather than forming advice to investors or businesses. As well as summarising sector-specific investment policies (notably investment exclusions), it lists five areas against which companies are monitored: responsible employment practices, best corporate governance practice, conscientiousness with regard to human rights, sustainable environmental practice and sensitivity towards the communities in which business operates.

The Methodist Church

Methodism, which emerged out of Anglicanism in the eighteenth century through the activities of John Wesley and others, has throughout its history maintained a keen awareness of ethics in business and economic life. In the US, the General Board of Pension and Health Benefits of the United Methodist Church manages about $15 billion of assets (according to its 2009 annual report). It restricts investment in alcoholic beverages, tobacco, gambling, pornography, defence and the violation of social principles. The social principles include human rights violations, abusive labour practices (including exploitation of child labour), damage to the environment and unethical business practices. In the UK, the Methodist Church has about £1.2 billion of investments managed by the Central Finance Board of the Methodist Church (CFB), which is advised by the Joint Advisory Committee on the Ethics of Investment (JACEI). The CFB website lists policy statements on the following areas: alcohol, caste discrimination, children's issues, climate change, financial intermediaries, the food industry, Israel and Palestine, the media, military-exposed companies, contractors supplying military and security services, mining companies and other extractive industries, Nestlé, prisons and voting at company annual general meetings.[5]

Islam

Islam has distinct and important ethical principles that are applicable to business, including investment banking. There has also been a significant growth in Islamic banking. Islam has developed distinctive banking arrangements, based on Shariah principles.

Islam places a high importance on ethical values in business, notably truthfulness and honesty, and requires clarity and openness in contracts. For example, it says in the Qu'ran:

> And do not mix the truth with falsehood or conceal the truth while you know it. (2:42)

Business or commerce feature prominently in Islamic religious texts, including the Qu'ran, and Islamic finance is now established as a major source of global finance, based on Islamic laws and rules relating to finance. As with the other Abrahamic faiths, the texts were written before the foundation of modern capitalism, and consequently the application of some texts can be interpreted differently by different scholars.

Islamic investment has prohibitions on investment in alcohol, tobacco, pornography, pork products and may also impose restrictions on gambling, armaments and some financial institutions.

Islam forbids all harmful drugs, including alcohol and (less clear-cut) tobacco. Alcohol is described as *haram* or forbidden. Tobacco is generally considered either *haram* or *makruh* (strongly disliked). Tobacco can be less clear-cut for many religions, as its use in many areas of the world post-dates primary religious texts. Some sectors are subject to ethical concerns on the grounds of causing harm, without being specifically proscribed in religious texts. Differing approaches to tobacco and defence reflect differing scholarly opinion. As with different Christian denominations, different Islamic traditions have varying approaches to investment screening.

Islamic investment may also prohibit investment in highly leveraged companies. Both the FTSE and the Dow Jones Islamic indices impose restrictions on investing in companies whose debt exceeds certain thresholds, although they use varying tests. Dow Jones applies a threshold of 33 per cent against three measures: total debt divided by trailing 24-month market capitalisation, the sum of a company's cash and interest-bearing securities divided by trailing 24-month market capitalisation, and accounts receivable divided by trailing 24-month average market capitalisation. FTSE applies a threshold, currently of 33 per cent, to the ratio of gross interest-bearing debt to total assets.

Shariah finance has distinctive features. These include risk-sharing – a profit can only be earned if a risk is shared – and a ban on interest: usury (*riba*) is prohibited, and the typical characteristic of Shariah finance is that interest payments are not made. A fee can be paid, if properly structured, for the use of capital or assets. Banks offering Islamic banking services have committees of Shariah scholars who advise on the implementation of Shariah. Different committees can reach different conclusions on some issues, and the implementation can change over time. Both Dow Jones and FTSE now have Shariah or Islamic indices.

One of the five pillars of Islam is *zakat*, charitable giving. This is a central tenet for Muslims, but one that is separate from investment.

In some cases, Shariah finance has been developed to mirror conventional financing techniques. For example, this occurs with project finance. In project financing (*Ijara*), instead of earning interest, Islamic financing institutions or vehicles may take control of assets and charge a lease for their usage. Sometimes, such charges appear similar to equivalent interest charges under conventional project finance.

Overall, Islam shares many areas of concern within business ethics with the other Abrahamic faiths, especially in ethical investment. Ethical investment is an area where there is significant common ground between Islam, Judaism and Christianity.

Judaism

In Judaism, ethical concerns restrict investment in a number of sectors. In the Jewish scriptures, there are clear injunctions regarding commercial behaviour, notably regarding contracts. The Torah presents laws regarding fair dealing and openness. Also, usury is prohibited in lending to Jews, but not to others. Other Jewish texts, including the Talmud and the Midrash, give significant guidance on day-to-day issues affecting people, which Jewish scholars are able to interpret with relevance to modern life.

In addition, there is a strong ethical obligation within certain traditions in Judaism for Jews to support Israel, which may include support through investments, where this is possible.

There is not an established "market" offering of investment products for Jewish investors, with specific screening applied in line with Judaism. Judaism prohibits investment in sectors that cause harm, notably alcohol, tobacco and armaments, as well as sectors relating to religious restrictions, notably foods considered unclean (pork products and shellfish).

Rabbi Dr Asher Meir of the Business Ethics Center in Jerusalem, in the "Jewish Values Based Investment Guide"[6] states that "In Jewish tradition, the highest form of charity is to make a business partnership with a potentially needy person; conversely, investments that patently promote anti-social activities are prohibited." Dr Meir proposes four guidelines for socially responsible investment (writing specifically for charities and communal organisations): avoiding investments contrary to the mission of the organisation (e.g., a charity); avoiding investments that could be viewed as condoning wrongdoing; co-operating with other groups to promote socially responsible investment; and where there is a conflict between prudent investment and socially responsible investment, consideration of how to resolve the conflicts in line with the organisation's mission.

Hinduism and Buddhism

There has been limited specific application of Buddhist and Hindu ethics to practical investment issues in international markets. In 2008, Dow Jones launched a series of "Dharma Indexes". With advice from a committee of experts, the indexes prohibited investment in both specific sectors and individual companies. Prohibited sectors included aerospace and defence, brewers, casinos and gaming, pharmaceuticals and tobacco. Companies that had activities which included alcohol production, adult entertainment, animal testing and genetic modification of agricultural products were prohibited.[7] The Dharma Indexes were intended to represent both Hindu and Buddhist ethics. The indexes are no longer active.

A short summary of the central teachings of Hinduism and Buddhism relevant to business ethics is set out below (although we note that both Hinduism and Buddhism encompass a range of different traditions, and generalisations regarding their teachings cannot be fully accurate).

Hinduism

Hinduism has developed a detailed set of metaphysical and ethical rules and values. Some of these share common influences with Western traditions.

Hindu ethics centre on *karma* (action) and *dharma* (duty). The Vedanta (or scriptures) does not deal directly with modern business issues, but does give detailed codes for ethical living. The Bhagavad Gita (literally the Song of the Lord) sets out a list of 26 virtues in Krishna's advice to the great warrior Arjuna (Krishna is an incarnation of the god Vishnu). Overall, Krishna sets out Arjuna's responsibility to his *dharma*, or duty – *dharma* is a fundamental concept in Hindu ethics. The 26 virtues include: to be peaceful, charitable, simple, clean, mild-mannered, magnanimous, saintly, equitable, truthful, obedient, merciful, to surrender the fruits of one's actions to God and avoid greediness, to be determined, steady, concise, expert, eloquent, friendly, compassionate, grave, humble, respectful and sober.

By implication, the application of Hindu ethics to investment banking would require bankers to do their duty (*dharma*) effectively, being successful as investment bankers, while carrying out their work with good or virtuous actions, such as truthfulness and openness.

Buddhism

Buddhism is concerned centrally with the self (*atman*). Central tenets of Buddhism are compassion and avoiding harm. This leads to concern for the world, people and all living creatures.

One of the central tenets of Buddhism, the Four Noble Truths, can be taken to refer to the Noble Eightfold Path. One aspect of this Path is "right livelihood". Based on the Noble Eightfold Path, Buddhism would proscribe investing or working in businesses involved with defence/armaments, exploitation of people, meat products, alcohol and tobacco and products that cause damage to the planet or living creatures (including contributing to climate change).

Sector exclusions for investment banks

Can an investment bank or investment banker have ethical objections to advising, supporting or dealing in companies engaged in activities that can be viewed as unethical? There are a number of institutions, both religious and secular, which proscribe investment in areas as diverse as tobacco, alcohol, firearms and defence, pornography, usury, abortion and baby milk. Interestingly, the viewpoint of most major religions is similar on many of these issues. The three Abrahamic faiths in particular have a high level of commonality in teaching in these areas.

It is interesting that ethical investment groups, notably those connected with major faith groups, have specific policies aimed at individual business sectors – indeed, this is the major area of concern for faith-based investment groups – but investment banking codes of ethics do not even discuss such concerns. There is a cogent argument that it is not up to individual companies to make judgements on the ethics of potential clients (or suppliers), but that ethical concerns in society are reflected in legislation. There are obvious shortcomings to this approach, not least the clear gap between legally prohibited activities and those avoided by ethical investment organisations, both secular and religious.

A number of religious groups set out detailed views on investment restrictions from an ethical perspective. The Church of England, through the EIAG, advises a multi-billion pound portfolio of equity investments, and sets out its investment restrictions in a series of policy documents.[8] These cover: defence, pornography, stem cell research, gambling, weekly collected home credit (seen as usurious) and alcohol. Each of these policies restricts the Church of England's investment in these areas. Restrictions are based on a threshold of revenue (such as 10% or 25% of revenue derived from a specific proscribed activity), although the policy papers do not explain the rationale in detail for specific thresholds. In addition, the EIAG's "Statement of Ethical Investment Policy" (July 2010) states that the Church of England's investment bodies may "avoid investment in companies whose management practices they judge to be unacceptable". This point is of particular importance from an ethical perspective: it is moving away from a purely prescriptive approach, and applying ethical judgement to the scrutiny of investee companies.

There are differences between denominations and between countries in how exclusions are implemented. This can be seen by looking at the Methodist approach to excluding alcohol from investment in the UK and in the US.

The Methodist Church in both the UK and the US publishes its investment policies. The Central Finance Board of the Methodist Church in the UK also publishes policy documents relating to specific sectors that are of ethical concern. The policy document on "Alcohol Related Companies"[9] states that the Methodist Central Finance Board divested from a food retailer when its alcohol-related sales rose above 20 per cent.

The General Board of Pension and Health Benefits of the United Methodist Church in the US states in its Investment Strategy Statement that it should not knowingly make investments in any company whose core business is making "alcoholic beverages" or who achieves more than 10 per cent of its "gross revenues" from "distributing, selling or marketing alcoholic beverages". Interestingly, although the same denomination of the same religion, these two different Methodist organisations appear to apply different thresholds to their investments when considering alcohol. In addition to showing an inconsistency, this may show the complexity of applying ethical screening to large (often international) organisations.

The United Methodist Investment Strategy Statement provides for exemptions to sector-based exclusions, including for emerging market commingled equity pools (provided they do not exceed 10% of the value of the funds). This exemption is presumably based around practical expediency. It would suggest that the investment exemptions are not all "categorical imperatives".

Governments

In addition, there are Governments that may be viewed as oppressive by ethical investors, where some organisations may choose not to do business or invest. There are ethical objections to supporting "oppressive" regimes. The definition of such regimes is not normally straightforward. In addition, it can at times be more harmful to withdraw investment from a country than to continue to operate there.

Lending, usury and interest payments

Given the common nature of lending within investment banking, we have looked specifically at religious concerns regarding lending, and whether they would affect investment banks.

All three Abrahamic faiths have strictures against usury, and lending in general, although these have been interpreted in differing ways between and within the faiths over time. The Abrahamic faiths all place restrictions on some forms of charging interest, whether all lending (Islam) or forms of usury (Christianity and Judaism). In Christianity, lending was prohibited in the early church and for much of the Middle Ages.

In the US, there are in some states specific laws proscribing usury, but there is no federal restriction. In the EU, including the UK, there is no specific law against usury.

It is unlikely that an investment bank would be in the position to charge a genuinely usurious interest rate; certainly even coupon levels in mezzanine finance fall very significantly below thresholds for usury where legal restrictions exist. Companies using investment banking services are unlikely to be in the position of borrowing at above interest rates of circa 30 per cent. An investment bank is unlikely to wish to lend to very high-risk propositions.

Thresholds

The major religions share common concerns over the ethics of investment in a number of sectors that they believe cause harm to individuals or society – notably alcohol, defence, tobacco, gambling and pornography.

The way that religious ethical concerns are managed varies greatly. Many large, organised religious denominations offer support to companies in these sectors, for example by providing industrial chaplains, and many members of organised religious denominations work in these sectors. The investment arms of religious denominations in many cases limit investment in these sectors, but not in a uniform way. Investment exclusions are in most cases managed by applying a test on the percentage of revenue derived from proscribed activities, typically of between 10 per cent and 25 per cent.

Ethical implications for investment banks

- The approach to business ethics by the major religions reflects a global interest in ethical concerns by a significant proportion of the world's population. The level of commonality regarding sectors of concern is very high. Religious attitudes to business ethics may in some way come to influence both legislation and perceptions of investment banks.
- A lack of consistency among religious organisations involved in ethical investment would suggest that it would be difficult – and possibly unnecessary – for an investment bank to elect to apply a rigorous ethical screen for companies involved in unethical sectors, although this

would not be impossible. It would be more important to do so when issuing a prospectus for a capital raising, as a prospectus goes out in the investment bank's name, and indicates support by an investment bank for a particular company. It would be more straightforward to apply this approach to an advisory business, where institutional investors may expect comprehensive coverage of an index, than to a capital markets business.

- Although sector-based screening may not be necessary for an investment bank, it would nonetheless be desirable. Ethically, it is important that investment banks should acknowledge and consider the issues raised by concerns over the ethical nature of activities carried out in ethically questionable sectors. This issue should be discussed in an investment bank's Code of Ethics.
- Religion is important in relation to cultural awareness business ethics.

Chapter summary

- The world's major religions share ethical concerns over activities across a number of sectors, notably alcohol, tobacco, defence, gambling and pornography.
- As investment banking activities have become the object of closer scrutiny, involvement in sectors that are ethically proscribed due to the harm they cause could become an area of scrutiny and concern.
- Religions have long-standing approaches to ethics, including business ethics. Religious ethics form a major part of a broader understanding of ethical issues.
- There are differences between religions, between denominations and between countries in their approach to ethical investment.
- The major religions tend to proscribe investment across a number of sectors that are regarded as causing harm to individuals or society, including alcohol, tobacco, defence and pornography. The way these investment restrictions are implemented is not uniform.
- Faith leaders have commented on the financial crisis. The Archbishop of Canterbury, Rowan Williams, said that economic activity "is subject to the same moral considerations as all other activities". Pope Benedict XVI, in *Caritas in Veritate*, stated that "Every economic decision has a moral consequence."
- There are ethical objections to supporting "oppressive" regimes, although the definition of an "oppressive regime" is not always straightforward.

- All three Abrahamic faiths have strictures against usury, and lending in general, although these have been interpreted in differing ways between the faiths over time.
- It would be difficult, but not impossible, for investment banks to apply a sector-based screen to their activities. This would be ethically desirable, but does not appear to be essential.
- Considerations regarding sectors of ethical concern should be raised in the investment bank's Code of Ethics.

Is a religious approach to ethics relevant to investment banking? Do investment banks have anything to learn from areas of common concern across the major religions?

5

The Two Opposing Views of Investment Banking Ethics: Rights vs Duties

In Chapter 3, we proposed that deontological ethics should be of primary importance in investment banking. We also identified five key questions that should inform ethical decision-making. Two of these, grounded in deontological ethics, are as follows: who are the stakeholders, and what duties are they owed? and what rights are relevant in the situation, and what bearing will they have in making a decision? The high-profile investigation of Goldman Sachs over the marketing of ABACUS, a mortgage-backed security, highlights these two questions. In particular, as the following comments suggest, a key ethical issue in investment banking is what weight should be given to duties to stakeholders relative to a firm's rights?

> *A Wall Street culture that, while it may once have been focused on serving clients and promoting commerce, is now all too simply self-serving. The ultimate harm is not just to clients poorly served by their investment banks. It's to all of us.* Senator Carl Levin, 27 April 2010, statement to the Senate Permanent Subcommittee on Investigations.
>
> *[T]he nature of the principal business in market making is that we are the other side of what our clients want to do.* Lloyd Blankfein, CEO of The Goldman Sachs Group Inc., 27 April 2010, testimony to the Senate Permanent Subcommittee on Investigations.

This exchange exposes a fundamental difference regarding the role of an investment bank, and a resulting difference in opinion as to how ethics should be applied in investment banking. This can be summarised as **a clash between the duties of an investment bank (to its clients) and its**

rights (and those of its shareholders and employees) to exploit *inter alia* intellectual property. **The reconciliation of conflicting rights and duties is at the heart of understanding ethics in investment banking.**

Putting aside the specific issue of the now infamous ABACUS 2007-AC1, the questions posed by Senator Carl Levin and the answers and testimony given by Goldman Chairman and CEO Lloyd Blankfein at the US Senate Permanent Subcommittee on Investigations (April 2010)[1] highlighted two opposing views of the role of investment banks: is an investment bank the prime orchestrator of a market, or is it just one of a number of market participants?

These differing perspectives also highlight alternative views of the overall nature of deontological ethics in investment banking: ethics based on duties, and ethics based on rights. Depending on how the role of an investment bank is understood in the market, a number of different conclusions can be reached on such fundamental issues as to whom an investment bank owes an ethical duty of care and, by extension, to specific questions relating to the ethics of markets, such as whether insider dealing is ethical or unethical.

The situation on which Mr Blankfein was questioned by Senator Levin relates, among others, to a civil fraud suit filed by the SEC[2] (Goldman settled the suit without admitting liability). Senator Levin told Mr Blankfein: "And you want people to trust you. I would not trust you." As discussed in Chapter 1, trust in counterparties is often cited as one of the key ethical differentiators of "markets", and a loss of trust in a major market counterparty in the way suggested by Senator Levin might indicate significant failings – both ethical and commercial.

The view that an investment bank very much orchestrates activity in the market and therefore has obligations that go beyond those relating only to participation has profound ethical consequences.

Conversely, Mr. Blankfein and other current and former Goldman executives have described Goldman's role as a "market maker" as very much a single market participant among numerous others.

A market maker is a market participant that offers prices at which it will buy and sell securities. A market maker makes a profit from the difference between the price it offers to buy (the "bid" price) and the price it offers to sell (the "offer" price). A market maker may also make a profit by taking a decision that a security is overvalued or undervalued and retaining a long or short position on its trading book. At the same time, the market maker is risking its capital, as many securities have prices that can move in a day by more than the difference between the bid and offer prices.

In contrast, an "agent" acts on behalf of other market participants and is paid a commission but does not take principal risk.

Defining the role of an investment bank in the market and its ethical position

The question of whether an investment bank is (normally) a market orchestrator or market participant – and both cannot be correct – can be summarised by one fundamental issue: is the investment bank, acting as a market maker, in a unique position, that is, a position to require market counterparties to trade with it? Even for a market maker with a strong market share, the major securities markets are highly competitive, at least as far as big-cap issues are concerned. The position of any specific investment bank in the major equity markets (such as NYSE or the London Stock Exchange) is not that of a quasi-monopoly, which ethically would require protection for clients (although this may not be the case in certain niche markets, or for trading in illiquid securities). An investment bank's clients – when trading in most liquid securities – can choose which investment bank to deal through. This can be different for trading in the securities of a small-cap stock where there may be only a small number of market makers (in such cases, the market maker is less likely to be one of the major investment banks, and investors may have more choice of stock in which to invest). **A market maker is not in a unique and privileged position in the market.**

It is also important to understand whether an investment bank, when acting as a market maker, is behaving as an investor and therefore should be treated as an investor, or whether it could arguably be treated differently. In one sense a market maker is an investor, in that it will own shares; however, the primary activity of a market maker is to derive a profit from offering firm or fixed prices to buy and sell. Therefore, although an investment bank is not in a unique position, **its behaviour is not that of an investor,** in that a market maker's ownership of shares is often very transitory and shares are not held as an investment as a matter of normal business practice. A market maker is not generally seeking to make a return from an increase in the value of the shares, but from providing "liquidity" to the market (the capital required to hold shares on its books as a result of offering a firm price for securities). Acting as a market marker, an investment bank will hold securities, normally for a very limited time (perhaps for a few hours, or even less). At times, it may hold them for significantly longer, but this is likely to be very much when it is taking an investment view on the securities concerned, and thus goes beyond "pure" market-making. In some jurisdictions, there may be tax advantages to holding shares as a market maker, even if in reality a shareholding may be part of a proprietary trading position.

The question of how an investment bank is viewed – as one of a number of market participants or alternatively as an orchestrator of the market – will influence how investment banks are expected to deal ethically with trading counterparties, whether fee-paying clients or non-fee-paying customers. Market-making is a different activity to investing. However, a market maker is trading with investors, and the terms of a trade need to be fair to both parties. It is relevant to note that counterparties will themselves generally be sophisticated and well resourced, and include institutional investors and hedge funds as well as other market makers.

Although an investment bank acting as a market maker does not behave as an investor, it is a market participant and does not occupy a unique and privileged position in the market. An investment bank structuring and issuing securities would be expected to have different ethical duties than when acting as a market maker.

Rights-based or duty-based ethics

Ethical analysis of an economic or industrial sector can be looked at within both a "rights-based" and a "duty-based" deontological framework.

An investment bank has a "right" to utilise its own intellectual property and market capabilities (including distribution, trading and so on), which may be the result of detailed analysis, market knowledge and the ability and resources to distribute securities. At the same time, it will have a "duty" to act ethically towards other market participants, notably its clients (fee-paying) and customers (non-fee-paying), which can be described as a "duty of care". In some cases, an investment bank's rights may conflict with its duties.

Interpretation of the investment bank's duty of care to its clients is not straightforward. Although we would argue that on a purely rights-based approach to ethics, an investment bank should be able to profit from its intellectual property, the implications of the duty of care vary according to the different activities of the investment bank. For example, the duty of care falls short of requiring the investment bank to disclose its intellectual property in all circumstances: an investment bank acting as a market maker would not be ethically required to disclose its underlying motivation for trading (such as its book position) but when an investment bank is acting as a principal to structure and sell securities, disclosure of intellectual property, such as its own view of the securities, would ethically be required. An investment bank ethically should not develop and sell its own securities if it believes these securities are substantially flawed, such as being materially overvalued.

Normally, it is ethical for an investment bank to retain its insights for its own use, for example to inform its own market-making and trading strategies. Of course, in circumstances where an investment bank does in fact divulge its own intellectual property, its clients will have their own views of the value of the securities, and may not in any case share the investment bank's views.

It should not be forgotten that investment banks continue to owe fiduciary duties to their shareholders – these duties are especially relevant for quoted companies, which include a number of major integrated investment banks as well as universal banks. The minority shareholders of an investment bank, who would not be expected to have direct board representation, have interests that the boards of the investment banks are required to protect. An alternative way of expressing an investment bank's right to monetise or capitalise on its intellectual property is by setting this within the framework of ethical "duties": to say that an investment bank has a duty of care to its shareholders to use its intellectual property effectively. However, on its own this concept is broad and could be extended to a range of activities that are likely to breach other ethical duties. The right to utilise intellectual property must be constrained by the duty of care to clients. In addition, if the right to use intellectual property is expressed as a duty, the way in which conflicts between a duty to shareholders and a duty to clients should be managed needs to be understood. From an ethical perspective, the duty of care to shareholders should not override the duty of care to clients.

As a largely "people-based" activity, investment banking centres on the ability of an investment bank's employees to create trading or transaction ideas of various types, for the bank or for its clients, and to execute them. Unless employees are taking part in some abusive and unethical practice, such as using price-sensitive information, there is no clear ethical argument why an investment bank cannot trade on the back of its own ideas. This type of trading can include simply buying or selling shares, or structuring investment vehicles.

Markets require liquidity and market makers who are prepared to offer firm prices in order for the markets themselves to operate effectively (a "firm" price is one at which a market maker is committed to trade if a counterparty wishes to do so), therefore market makers must be allowed to develop their own views on the value of securities.

Alternatively, in a duty-based approach to ethics, an investment bank has a simple duty of care to its clients. This involves accurately describing securities or investment structures, and carrying out the execution of deals effectively. Even where an investor is not the (fee-paying) client of the investment bank, the investment bank still ethically has some form of duty of care (even if not a "fiduciary" duty).

It is worth drawing a distinction between the duty of care owed to two different categories of client, which we will refer to as, in one case, "clients" and, in the other, "customers". The duty owed to a client (who is paying the investment bank a fee) and that owed to customers (who buy from an investment bank, but without paying fees) may differ. In practice, many "clients" will also be "customers", depending on the specific activity being undertaken. An investment bank may not have a "fiduciary" duty of care to a customer (under this definition of a customer), but, nonetheless, from an ethical perspective it has similar duties to other commercial enterprises (in the same way as a retailer) to describe products accurately, and not to mislead.

Fiduciary duties would not be expected to conflict with ethical duties in most circumstances. As has been seen in a number of instances during the financial crisis, failing to take ethical issues into account can cause a major loss in shareholder value. Ethical behaviour may in fact protect shareholder value.

The approach taken to defend Goldman's position regarding ABA-CUS can also be explained in part by moral relativism, applying ethical standards in the context of what was common practice at the time in the market for mortgage-backed securities. This approach, although used in a number of contexts, has clear limitations and is not necessarily supported by other ethical approaches, and is one that does not stand scrutiny from an ethical perspective.

It is interesting to note in the context of the interchange between Senator Levin and Mr Blankfein that the Goldman Code of Business Conduct and Ethics does in fact proscribe any "unethical" behaviour. It does not, however, explain how to define what is and is not unethical in a way that is practically helpful in this context (see Codes of Ethics in Chapter 3).

Reconciling the conflict between rights and duties

In most contexts where ethics are carefully applied, there are some conflicts between different frameworks or approaches. The conflict here, between an investment bank's right to use its intellectual property and its duty to its customers, is not one that can be resolved easily, but it is capable of being managed. As a comparison, a hospital or health care department may not have the funds or infrastructure to care for all its patients at all times in the way in which it would wish to do, and so is forced to set priorities.

An investment bank does not simply have a choice over whether it should take a rights-based approach or duty-based approach to ethical decisions. For an investment bank, the resolution comes from a combination of setting key ethical rules, understanding which rights or duties take precedence and transparency.

Limits should be set by defining a series of clear rules (categorical imperatives, to use the phrase developed by Kant) that cannot be breached. These may include, for example, existing rules, such as a rule that a salesman will not give incorrect information in answer to a specific direct question.

In the absence of a breach of the categorical imperatives, it needs to be understood whether rights or duties take precedence. Where there is a conflict, it is important to resolve a clash between duties and rights. In different circumstances, either ethical rights or duties could in theory have precedence, for example in cases relating to rights such as life and liberty. However, in investment banking, issues being dealt with relate to commercial issues, such as the ability to make a profit from intellectual property, rather than cases related to more fundamental rights, such as the right to life or liberty. In investment banking, the key ethical action is to identify whether a right is in conflict with a duty. Given that investment banking rights are unlikely to relate to fundamental rights, where there is a breach of a duty in order to exercise an ethical right, an investment bank should not try to exercise its right. From an ethical perspective, **the specific *duties* of an investment bank have to take precedence over specific *rights***, in part because the stated rationale for the investment bank's existence depends on its ability to serve its clients; however, the existence of duties does not in itself prevent an investment bank from exercising its rights. A compliance framework, or a process of communication to clients or other stakeholders, is unlikely to change the requirement for ethical duties to take precedence over ethical rights where there is such a conflict.

It is important to be transparent (that is, informing clients where appropriate) when rights-based and duty-based ethics are in conflict. Transparency is not adequate in itself, but it is important for an investment bank to explain to its various categories of clients and customers how they will be treated, including in circumstances where the investment bank faces a conflict between ethical rights and duties. In practice, this is problematic, as a good (by which we mean effective) salesman is hardly likely to indicate that his clients are not the highest priority for him.

Ethical standards in on-market trading

Investment banks have a clear duty to support established markets, or their own activities are invalidated (ethically and practically). Legislation and regulation differentiate between on-market and off-market activity.

This legislation can present apparent anomalies: legislation in major markets (including the US and the European Union) falls short of proscribing all insider dealing and "market abuse", specifically where they are outside what the EU refers to as "qualifying markets" and "qualifying instruments".

Legislation relating to insider dealing offers a number of inconsistencies. In some markets and in relation to some securities insider dealing is illegal. However, in recognised markets, some forms of insider dealing are specifically allowed even where it is otherwise illegal, such as stakebuilding ahead of a public offer for a controlling interest in a company in the UK under the Takeover Code (The City Code on Takeovers and Mergers). As set out in Chapter 6, insider dealing is unethical by some specific ethical standards, but is in fact legal in some circumstances, instruments and jurisdictions. The European Market Abuse regime only covers "qualifying investments", and, for example, excludes trading in some (normally physical) assets.

As discussed in Chapter 1, a market relies on ethical behaviour from market participants if it is to function effectively. However, at the same time, a market can only function if there are different views between market participants. Consequently, while markets can be "efficient" and it is understood that all participants are seeking to profit, there can also be unequal economic outcomes to market activity (one counterparty may profit and another lose from a trade). Preventing outcomes where some participants incur losses may be an attractive ideal, but it is not practical and not ethically required. It also gives rise to moral hazards.

If an investment bank is by its nature a market counterparty, and is expected by its customers and the market operators to take risks, it is difficult to expect the investment bank to behave towards all market counterparties as if they are clients, and to act so as to always protect its counterparties' interests. However, where an investment bank is selling securities, either for commission to existing clients or to non-commission-paying customers, the investment bank would be expected to deal fairly, and to make appropriate disclosure, so that its products can be understood and therefore valued properly.

In normal market trading, it is common market practice to deal on the basis of well-understood assumptions, which do not need to be specified for each transaction – for example, when selling a share in a company, it is accepted that the share is equivalent to other shares normally traded, and that settlement terms are those under normal market rules. In this context, any difference from the norm needs to be disclosed in advance of a deal being agreed.

Applying ethical standards to off-market trading

The ethics of both on and off-market trading need to be considered as separate but related issues. For example, CDOs and CDSs (credit default swaps) have (to date) not been traded on recognised exchanges. Their position is therefore very different to that of equities traded on the NYSE or the London Stock Exchange. The ethical duty of an investment bank when trading off-market also depends on how it treats its market-related activities. There is an ethical duty to uphold the standards of market behaviour when trading on-market, but this does not necessarily apply to off-market trading. To what extent, then, do the ethics of on-market trading apply off-market?

The question of whether there is a duty to maintain market standards of behaviour when dealing off-market is complex, especially in an environment when regulatory authorities, legislation and Governments do not require such behaviour in all circumstances, and market participants do not exhibit such behaviour in all cases. Maintaining ethical behaviour off-market therefore could come at the cost of forsaking profits.

It is clear that investment banks have an ethical duty to support proper market conduct when dealing on-market. This duty must extend in some circumstances to behaviour off-market.

Duties to support markets

Ethical arguments for investment banks supporting markets are similar to well-understood arguments for the payment of taxes. Citizens of a country benefit from the existence of a stable Government, in diverse ways, which, although they vary from country to country, might include security, health care, education, infrastructure and so forth. Citizens who benefit from such provision have a duty to "support" their Government through paying taxes, as well as by obeying laws. Likewise, investment banks benefit from the existence of and their participation in markets, and therefore should support them, which includes obeying market rules. Without established and effective markets, investment banks would be unable to distribute and trade securities effectively. Supporting markets involves engaging in forms of business conduct that are conducive to orderly (and efficient) markets.

In general, investment banks have a duty to maintain ethical standards of behaviour when dealing both on-market and off-market. Investment banks need to consider carefully how to implement this duty, as market standards of conduct are a mixture of ethics, legislation, regulation and common practice, which have different ethical values. There are two specific circumstances where market standards of behaviour may not be required off-market: first, some forms of behaviour required to support specific markets stem from following common practice, which may not have an ethical value; and second, some forms of behaviour follow specific regulation or legislation relating to particular markets, which may not be ethically required, for example, where behaviour is only ethically required from a utilitarian perspective, in that it supports a particular rule, but is not supported from a virtue perspective. Whereas there may be an ethical duty to support Governments and markets and therefore follow applicable legislation, and there should be a presumption that an investment bank has a duty to adopt such standards off-market, such a duty does not automatically impose specific ethical duties on off-market behaviour.

Given that an investment bank's behaviour off-market may influence other market participants, an investment bank should consider the ethics of its off-market standards of conduct in the light of its duties to support Governments and markets. Ethically, if off-market behaviour were to undermine the effectiveness of the markets, the investment bank would have a duty to change its conduct.

There are other situations in which an investment bank would have a duty to behave in line with its market conduct when dealing off-market:

- If this is what it has led its clients and customers to believe it will do.
- If normal off-market standards of conduct are clearly unethical.

Is behaviour always either ethical or unethical, or can it be ambivalent?

Some forms of behaviour are mechanistic or procedural, and it can be difficult to assign any especial ethical value to them. Any product-structuring or outward-facing marketing activity could have an ethical dimension.

Advisory vs trading/capital markets

The advisory business of an investment bank faces significantly different day-to-day ethical issues from the trading and capital markets business. By definition, the ethical issues faced by an advisory business do not typically relate to the type of challenge highlighted above, of acting as a principal. However, all parts of an investment bank, including advisory activities, have to contend with ethical issues of trust and conflicts of interest. Issues affecting advisory activities, including conflicts of interest, and questions over frequent ethical concerns such as truth and misleading information are dealt with in Chapter 7.

Ethical implications for investment banks

- An investment bank has the right to utilise its intellectual property and infrastructure, but is constrained by duties: the duty of care to both clients (fee-paying) and customers (non-fee-paying); the duty to act honestly and not lie or mislead.
- Where rights are in conflict with duties, an ethical right cannot subjugate an ethical duty to another group of stakeholders.
- From an ethical perspective, there is a duty of care to all customers, not just the fiduciary duty to fee-paying clients.
- Investment banks have an ethical duty to uphold market standards of behaviour, which includes following applicable legislation and regulation. However, simply following normal market practice is not sufficient from an ethical perspective.
- Ethical standards of behaviour for trading on-market do not in all cases need to be applied off-market. This is because the ethical standards applied for on-market behaviour are in part based on legislation and regulation, some of which applies standards that do not stand up to ethical scrutiny; however, off-market trading nonetheless requires clear ethical standards.
- These standards are harder for an investment bank to apply, as they do not always relate clearly to legislation.

Chapter summary

- What weight should be given to ethical duties to stakeholders relative to a firm's ethical rights?
- The exchanges at the US Senate Permanent Subcommittee on Investigations (April 2010) regarding ABACUS highlighted two opposing views

concerning the role of investment banks: is an investment bank the prime orchestrator of a market, or is it just one of a number of market participants?

- From an ethical perspective, an investment bank has the right to utilise its intellectual property and infrastructure, but is constrained by duties: the duty of care to both clients (fee-paying) and customers (non-fee-paying); the duty to act honestly and not lie or mislead.
- The existence of ethical rights cannot absolve an investment bank of its ethical duties.
- An investment bank's clients – when trading in most liquid securities – can choose which investment bank to deal through.
- Acting as a market marker, an investment bank will normally hold securities for a very limited time, and the investment bank will not behave like a typical "investor".
- Investment banks have a clear duty to support established markets, or their own activities are invalidated (ethically and practically). A market relies on ethical behaviour from market participants if it is to function effectively.
- Legislation concerning market behaviour is not always ethically consistent, for example regarding insider dealing.
- This makes determining ethical standards for off-market trading more difficult. Despite this, off-market trading requires clear ethical standards.
- It would be unethical for an investment bank to adopt practices in off-market trading if these were found to undermine confidence or encourage unethical behaviour in regulated markets, given the ethical duty to support markets.

Is it possible to reconcile an approach to investment banking ethics based on an investment bank's rights, with one based on its duties? Should an investment bank consider ethical issues before taking advantage of a legal loophole to enter a profitable trade?

6
Recent Ethical Issues in Investment Banking

The specific ethical issues that characterised the financial crisis included manipulating credit ratings, the mis-selling of securities, unauthorised trading and the short-selling of bank shares. In addition, there are long-standing ethical concerns regarding practices such as market manipulation and insider dealing. The ethical implications of these practices are not uniform – it would be difficult to objectively consider some of these activities to be unethical, whereas others are clearly unethical.

The financial crisis exposed a number of practices in investment banking that have been described as unethical. In addition, there are practices that have been prominent in the past which raise ethical concerns. This chapter looks at:

- Manipulating credit ratings
- Mis-selling securities
- Mis-selling in M&A
- Over-leverage
- Unauthorised trading
- Insider dealing
- Market manipulation and market abuse
- CDOs/CDSs and off-market trading
- Speculation
- Short-selling

Credit ratings

Flawed credit rating assessments were a significant contributing factor to the financial crisis. Rating securities as "investment grade" enabled them to be sold to a mass market of investors, creating a massive market for securities backed by sub-prime mortgages. These ratings were systemically flawed.

Credit ratings are determined by credit rating agencies, whose main purpose is to assess financial products so as to provide investors and others with the information required to assess what is a fair price for the products and what are the risks associated with them. A credit rating is issued by a credit rating agency, but is (normally) paid for by the issuer of the rated securities (rather than the investors).

Although investment banks do not issue credit ratings themselves, they are directly involved when an issuer is given a rating, either as the underwriter of the securities or by advising the issuer (the company issuing the securities) on the credit rating process. In addition, investment banks seek credit ratings for their own securities or complex securities, which they package and sell.

There was a widespread re-evaluation of the role of rating agencies and the risk of conflicts of interest in the wake of the Enron and WorldCom credit downgrades and bankruptcies. These bankruptcies were not alone, as there were a series of failures in both the telecoms/cable and the independent power producer sectors. In the case of Enron, there was notoriously a multi-notch downgrade to sub-investment grade status (28 November 2001), sometime after (energy) market counterparties had stopped accepting Enron credit risk. In the wake of these events, there was a SEC review of rating agencies. Interestingly, despite the UK's economic reliance on rating agencies, the UK did not carry out a similar detailed review, and still does not regulate rating agencies.

Given that there were only limited changes in ratings practice following the Enron/WorldCom defaults and the SEC review, it should not have come as a surprise that – at some stage – there was another systemic problem in calculating credit ratings. Both Lehman and Bear Stearns carried investment grade credit ratings right up until they failed, although it should be noted that some smaller rating agencies and ratings research organisations had already downgraded them to sub-investment grade status (a "downgrade" refers to a reduction in the recommended credit rating applied to the company).

Credit rating agencies came under severe criticism during the financial crisis, from the Financial Crisis Inquiry Commission in the US among others, because they rated many of the mortgage-based securities at the heart of the crisis as investment grade, including many at AAA – the highest rating – which seriously underestimated the risk associated with them.

Rating agencies are typically paid for each rating given and therefore have a business model that incentivises them to maximise the number of ratings given and preserve relationships with issuers of securities. From an ethical point of view, the inherent conflict of interest in the rating agency business model calls into question the trustworthiness of the agencies. As a consequence of systemically flawed credit ratings of mortgage-backed securities, important market and investment decisions were based on misinformation.

The failure of credit ratings to accurately assess risk across the investment banking sector, and, immediately previously, the housing sector, is not simply an ethical issue for investment banking, as it directly affects rating agencies, their regulators and Governments. However, investment banks have the expertise to manipulate credit ratings. Investment banks handle the issuance of large volumes of rated debt (frequently hiring staff from ratings agencies), and as well as packaging and issuing securities themselves they routinely provide advice to debt issuers on managing the credit ratings process. This leads to an ethical question on how far it is appropriate for an investment bank to "manage" a credit rating in order to get a desired outcome, both as a principal, and as an adviser. Ultimately, it is unethical to be complicit in a lie. The duty of care owed to a client, or the fiduciary duties of directors, would point to a bank working hard to ensure the best possible outcome from a ratings review, but falls short of deliberately misleading rating agencies through the manipulation of issuers' financial projections, which would be unethical.

Mis-selling – Securities

The mis-selling of goods and services has long been a moral – and legal – issue in business. From a deontological point of view, it raises issues of duties towards others and the rights of market participants to be treated fairly. Mis-selling can also distort markets, as market decisions are then based on misinformation. Mis-selling also diminishes trust – both in individual companies and in markets more generally. From a consequentialist point of view, market distortion is also an ethical concern as it leads to a misallocation of resources.

The type of mis-selling seen where products, which have been understood by an investment bank to be flawed in some way, have been sold, highlights problems with a bank's potential conflicts of interest.

There are numerous cases of the creation of seriously flawed financial products, by investment banks and others, which contributed to the financial crisis. Ethically, it is important to look at the intention as well as the consequences resulting from the sale of products that fail. Where the seller is aware that the product will fail, and the intention is to sell a flawed product, the sale is unethical. Where the sale of a flawed product results from a lack of understanding, this is primarily a question of competence rather than ethics. The financial crisis highlighted issues of both ethics and competence in the creation and sale of mortgage-backed securities.

Among the cases of alleged mis-selling of securities during the financial crisis is the charges made by the Securities and Exchange Commission (SEC) in the US against Goldman Sachs in relation to a synthetic CDO, ABACUS 2007-AC1.[1]

The SEC alleged that Goldman was paid by a hedge fund, Paulson & Co., to structure a transaction in which Paulson & Co. could take short positions against mortgage securities. The SEC alleged that Goldman did not disclose to investors that Paulson & Co. played "a significant role" in selecting securities in which ABACUS would invest. The SEC stated that investors in the ABACUS structure lost more than $1 billion. Internal emails by Goldman employees involved in structuring and selling the transaction appear to show serious concerns about its value. Goldman settled the civil case, agreeing to pay a fine of $550 million, without admitting or denying wrongdoing.

Goldman CEO, Lloyd Blankfein, in his testimony to the US Senate Permanent Subcommittee on Investigations (27 April 2010) explained that in this situation Goldman was a counterparty and not a fiduciary and therefore did not owe investors in ABACUS a duty of care. Mr Blankfein also stated that Goldman's clients did not care what Goldman's view might have been on the investment case. If a salesman was asked a direct question, he would nonetheless have a duty to respond honestly. Goldman, in focusing on "fiduciary" duty, appears to be taking a specifically legal view of a "duty of care". For reasons discussed in Chapter 3 and Chapter 7, we would argue that an investment bank's ethical duty of care should cover a wider group of clients or customers than those covered by its pure fiduciary responsibilities. In addition, it is possible that by behaving unethically, the value of an investment bank's reputation may be reduced.

The behaviour in such a case could be considered unethical on two related grounds: first, if the investment bank did not disclose information necessary for investors to understand the value of the investment they were buying; and, second, if the investment bank believed that the securities would fail.

Goldman's description of its role in the market in its appearance before the Senate hearing was noteworthy: it essentially described itself as another market participant or counterparty, that is, as trading securities rather than selling to clients. As such, Goldman could be seen as demonstrating that even the largest market participants can benefit from behaviour which in the longer term might reduce trust in markets (depending on how much trust it is assumed is put in markets anyway). An alternative conclusion, more consistent with Goldman's own statements, is that Goldman demonstrated behaviour consistent with a view that investment banks are no more than market participants, and should not be seen as, in any way, orchestrating or championing specific markets.

It is important to note that investment banks carry out a number of different activities, including selling securities that they own as well as selling securities on behalf of clients. These two different activities often involve selling securities to the same clients.

Mis-selling – M&A

In a corporate sales process, where a company is being sold, the asymmetry of information between seller and buyer provides an investment bank advising on a sale with the opportunity to present information to its benefit, including that regarding the level of "price tension" in the sales process. This can contribute to buyers overpaying for assets and as a result over-leveraging them.

As was seen the 2010–11 New York court case between Citi and Terra Firma over EMI (where Terra Firma unsuccessfully sued Citi regarding Terra Firma's acquisition of EMI), there are risks that investment banks may have, or be perceived to have, incentives to lie or deliberately mislead while engaged in corporate finance transactions, notably in the sale of a business. With fees for transactions based largely on success, and fees for sell-side advice often related to the price achieved, an investment bank may stand to be seriously affected by the outcome of a sales process. This conflict is heightened where a sell-side adviser is also financing a bidder for a business or asset.

Lying in a sales process is unethical. Deliberately misleading can be more complicated, but would also be considered unethical as it seeks to influence an outcome by obscuring the truth.

Over-leverage and loan-to-own

In most cases, a commercial decision to lend to a business is made on the basis of an assessment of the business's ability to service and ultimately repay a loan. Write-offs, resulting from non-performance of a loan, are the outcome of commercial decisions. Such write-offs do not normally have ethical connotations – within a portfolio of loans, some level of default will be expected. Over-leverage can result from a wide range of factors, such as a change in trading conditions associated with the general economic environment.

However, there are lending practices that may be unethical, including those associated with encouraging a debtor to incur greater indebtedness than is likely to be able to be serviced in order to profit from the situation, for example by assuming ownership without paying the element relating to equity in the capital structure, or lending beyond a retail customer's obvious ability to service a debt. The financial benefits of such types of practice will vary according to jurisdiction, depending *inter alia* on applicable insolvency laws.

Such loans, if made on a transparent basis, would not always be considered unethical, for example if they were made as some form of "emergency" finance once a company were in distress (such as DIP or Debtor in Possession finance).

Unauthorised trading

In setting out an ethical framework in Chapter 3, we highlighted the importance of values and virtuous behaviour, both individually and collectively, in business. Whilst mis-selling can be either an individual or collective ethical failure, unauthorised trading in investment banking focuses very much on the individual – although the culture and management structure of a firm may well be an important factor when it occurs. Such issues have been highlighted in several high-profile incidents.

On 5 October 2010, Jérôme Kerviel, a trader with Société Générale in Paris, was convicted for a series of unauthorised trades, which lost €4.9 billion. He was sentenced to five years' imprisonment (two of which were suspended) and fined €4.9 billion. The judge said that Mr Kerviel's trades had threatened the existence of Société Générale. Mr Kerviel's (unsuccessful) defence included the assertion that his superiors were aware of his trading.

There are a series of ethical issues raised by this case:

- Trading and making losses is not unethical (assuming there is no actual intention to cause losses, especially damaging ones). It is not in itself unethical to lose money or to live in poverty.
- Trading with no authorisation – risking someone else's capital without their permission is unethical. This is the case whether or not the individual trading intends to personally profit from the trades.
- Trading with informal authorisation, which is not properly recorded, would not necessarily be unethical, but could be damaging to the trader if the trades go wrong.

The issue of trading without a formal record of authorisation (the basis of Mr Kerviel's defence, which was not accepted by the judge) can be one primarily of internal processes within an investment bank. If there is a deliberate attempt to subvert internal processes, then the actions would be unethical.

There have been a number of high-profile cases involving rogue traders. One of these, Nick Leeson, in fact did bring about the demise of his employer, the relatively small (compared, for example, with the bulge bracket) but highly prestigious Barings Bank.

Although the ethical position would be complex regarding whether a trader was committing a specifically unethical act by trading without a formal record of authorisation if they had nonetheless been informally authorised to trade, the same would not be the case for the managers who gave the "informal" authorisation. This would clearly be a breach of internal risk-management processes. To do this would be unethical, as it would breach processes put in place specifically to protect the investment bank's, and therefore the shareholders', capital.

In drawing these differentiations, it is necessary to look not just at the outcome (assuming all the trading scenarios discussed above are equal in terms of their financial outcome), but to look also at the intention. As discussed in Chapter 3, there are varying ethical views on the importance of consequences and intentions. In the case of unauthorised trading, the outcome may appear ethically less important than the intention.

Insider dealing

Instances of insider dealing in financial services in the 1980s were one of the driving forces behind the development of business ethics. Again, the focus tends to be on individual behaviour – in this case how one makes use of certain information – but it, too, raises questions of business culture and how employee performance is incentivised.

Insider dealing has not been a major focus of analysis of the financial crisis. However, given its prominence as a financial crime, and some complex ethical issues it raises, it is examined here.

There are differing economic views on whether insider dealing is a harmful practice. It can harm market efficiency and create an unfair trading environment, thereby undermining general market confidence. However, it is sometimes described as a "victimless crime". Insider dealing can be seen as creating more efficient pricing, with the potential to give better pricing to counterparties in some circumstances (but also to give worse pricing in other circumstances).

Insider dealing is a crime in major markets. It was legal in the UK until the 1970s and remained legal in some jurisdictions, such as Japan and Italy, until the 1980s or 1990s.

The legal prohibition on insider dealing is not universal: there are both markets and instruments that are not covered by insider dealing laws, and there are specific exemptions where insider dealing is normally prohibited. Insider dealing is illegal on "recognised exchanges" or "qualifying markets". It remains legal in some markets when trading in instruments that are not exchange traded, such as some bank debt. The ambiguity over the legal status of insider dealing – illegal in some cases, not in others – makes the ethical position of insider dealing unclear.

Insider dealing is not unethical from all ethical standpoints – the ethical objections to insider dealing are primarily utilitarian, but also deontological: the rules regarding insider dealing relate to concerns over maintaining orderly markets. The existence of exemptions, and financial instruments that fall outside of insider dealing rules, raise questions over whether it can be seen as unethical from a "virtue" perspective. In circumstances where it is generally illegal, there are situations where some forms of insider dealing are nonetheless legal, reinforcing its sometimes ethically ambiguous position.

As well as being unethical from a utilitarian perspective in that it undermines markets, insider dealing could also be seen as unethical from a deontological (duty-based) perspective, in that it is contrary to the duty to support and uphold the markets in which an investment bank is a participant, and therefore there is a duty to uphold all rules relating to these markets.

From an ethical perspective, where insider dealing is based on the abuse of confidential or privileged information, it is also unethical from a virtue perspective – the question of abuse of information is more clear-cut than insider dealing itself.

The differentiation between a legal and an illegal act in this area can be very narrow. This, for example, can be the case with the difference between dealing on the basis of proprietary research and dealing on the basis of insider information, both of which may turn out to be based on the same belief.

The complexities of insider dealing laws and ethics lead to the conclusion that although insider dealing is not intrinsically wrong from all ethical perspectives, when looked at ethically insider dealing is ethically wrong on three grounds: first, in that it undermines the operation of markets, which have some ethical benefits in themselves; second, in that investment banks (and other market participants) have an ethical duty to uphold markets and market behaviour; and third, in that insider dealing would normally relate to the abuse of privileged or confidential information.

From this conclusion, it becomes questionable whether an investment bank could ethically justify engaging in or supporting insider dealing in some cases where it is nonetheless legal (e.g., in bank debt) while maintaining a restriction on insider dealing on recognised exchanges where it is illegal. The ethical objection on this basis would relate to the likelihood of abuse of privileged information and the general undermining of market standards of conduct, rather than ethical objections to insider dealing *per se*.

Insider dealing and equity research

The way that analyst research is used and disseminated by investment banks is primarily an issue of compliance with the law and regulation. However, there are ethical issues relating to the production of research that have complex ethical implications. These notably surround the production of research that may be price sensitive.

There is a real issue in this area confronting equity research departments and individual analysts: at what stage does proprietary research become market sensitive, and what are the ethical issues related to producing research that will be price sensitive?

Equity analysts aim to produce groundbreaking research that can move prices. When an analyst has produced such a piece of research, based on an investment bank's ethical right to profit from its intellectual property, the investment bank would have an ethical right to use this research in whatever way it felt was likely to maximise its value. Such research, where produced by a hedge fund or institutional investor (which also have research analysts carrying out similar work to equity analysts in investment banks) would be a legitimate basis on which to deal.

However, although not based on privileged or confidential information, research can be itself considered as price-sensitive information, and is therefore required to be "published" by being properly disseminated to the investment bank's clients. Failing to fully circulate such research, and instead initially circulating it to just a small close group of investors, perhaps via a "desk note", can be illegal.

In this case, the ethical position of the analyst and investment bank is, from a utilitarian perspective, to uphold market rules and laws and publish the research in accordance with applicable regulation, even though this may conflict with the ethical rights of the investment bank. This is also an ethical issue from a deontological perspective, as it relates to the investment bank's duty to uphold markets. In this case, the ethical duties of the investment bank, and utilitarian ethics, override the investment bank's ethical rights.

Conversely, the position of an equity analyst receiving information from a company insider would be more clear-cut from an ethical point of view. This issue, again relatively common, is governed by clear rules and laws governing price-sensitive information. In this case, the question of insider dealing is allied to the question of abuse of position or information, making this practice also unethical from a virtue perspective: that is, it is different from the case where an equity analyst has produced proprietary research in a way that could theoretically be done by numerous others.

Market manipulation and market abuse

Market manipulation

Although subject to detailed legislation and regulation proscribing specific activities, market manipulation can be much easier to achieve, yet more difficult to prove – and therefore more tempting – than insider dealing. Market manipulation involves creating an artificial move in a share price in order to profit from a trading opportunity.

There are numerous possible examples of market manipulation. One concerns Regal Petroleum, a company listed on the UK's Alternative Investment Market, the junior market of the London Stock Exchange. On 3 October 2008, a UK newspaper, the *Daily Telegraph*,[2] reported that Royal Dutch Shell had written to the Chairman of Regal Petroleum proposing to acquire the company. The company's shares had closed at 83 pence on 2 October, the previous day, and rose to close at 125 pence on 3 October, a rise of 51 per cent. The letter purportedly discussed a valuation of 300 pence per share. The story was rapidly denied by Regal, who issued a statement saying: "In response to press speculation this morning regarding a possible approach by Royal Dutch Shell plc to acquire Regal, the company confirms that no such approach has been received." Under rule 2.2 (c)[3] of the UK's Takeover Code, if Royal Dutch Shell had in fact made an approach, which had leaked and resulted in an "untoward movement" in share price, then it would have been Royal Dutch Shell who would have been required to make an announcement, rather than Regal. The fact that Regal issued a denial and no statement was made by Shell should have indicated that the story was untrue. The story turned out to be entirely fictional, but inspired a rise in share price, presumably providing a selling opportunity for the investor who had fabricated the story.

False rumours can also cause significant movements in the shares of major companies, but this is less likely to have such a meaningful impact on prices of large-cap comapnies, than it would for for small-cap companies; with greater liquidity, dedicated investor relations departments and retained brokers or ECM advisers, large-cap companies are able to dispel false information rapidly, in a way not always possible for small-cap companies. In addition, the capital required to move prices for large-cap companies would be much greater than for small caps.

Rumours can be used to move a share price to create an opportunity to trade profitably in a security. For example, as described above, an (unfounded) rumour of a takeover approach can be used to move a share price significantly. This is easiest to achieve in small-cap stock, but nonetheless is possible with big caps. There are numerous ways of doing this, some long-standing, some relatively novel. These include leaving messages on investors' internet forums as well as talking directly to market participants or journalists. Where market manipulation involves deliberately disseminating factually false information, this is always unethical behaviour.

There can, at times, be a fine line between normal investor relations activity and market manipulation. Although results statements and formal announcements from a company must be verified, the day-to-day discussion between a company and investors is not normally so tightly controlled. This can result in a company or its advisers giving out messages that are unduly positive in order to boost the share price. Like an investment banking pitch, investor relations activities that mislead are tantamount to lying and are therefore unethical.

Market abuse

"Market abuse" is a term used to describe legally proscribed activities that knowingly create a false market in a security. These practices, in some cases, cover not only already illegal activities, including insider dealing, but also activities that are banned in some jurisdictions under market regulations, such as disseminating false rumours. The ethical connotations of these forms of behaviour are sometimes complex.

The UK's FSA lists a series of specific abuses (FSA Code of Market Conduct MAR1):[4] insider dealing, improper disclosure, misuse of information, manipulating transactions, manipulating devices, dissemination, misleading behaviour and distortion (examples given below are taken from the FSA's Code of Market Conduct). These are set out in MAR1 as:

- Insider dealing, which covers using confidential information to trade in securities, as discussed above.
- Manipulating transactions involves carrying out securities trades in a way designed to give a false impression. Notably this could involve making a stock look more actively traded (most applicable to small-cap stocks) or carrying out trades immediately before the market closes, designed to show a misleading closing price.
- Manipulating devices include strategies such as "pump and dump" and "trash and cash". These involve taking a long or short position in a stock, and then disseminating a story that causes the stock to rise or fall (depending on whether the investor is long or short), before liquidating the position.
- Improper disclosure includes behaviour such as providing inside information in a social context or in a selective briefing of analysts.
- Dissemination of information includes spreading rumours or false information about a company.
- Misuse of information covers areas that abuse confidential information and which are not otherwise caught by insider dealing rules, such as dealing by an employee in the light of potential price-sensitive information gained as a result of their employment.

The FSA also gives examples of misleading behaviour and distortion that relate to the physical commodity sector, involving the movement of empty ships to falsely portray an indication of activity in commodity markets.

The practices described by the FSA in MAR1 are not unique to the capital markets, and in other sectors of the economy might not be considered illegal or even, in some circumstances, unethical. The FSA's Code of Market Conduct in itself has limited applicability – it only applies to "qualifying investments". Such investments are generally securities traded on recognised exchanges. The market abuse regime does not cover shares traded on unrecognised exchanges, or unquoted companies, or unlisted securities issued by quoted companies.

The different legal or regulatory strictures relating to other sectors, outside investment banking, change the ethical nature of the different types of market abuse in one crucial way: for investment banks that rely on markets, the ethics of engaging in activities proscribed for "qualifying instruments" or "qualifying exchanges" may vary when trading outside these areas. There are investment banks that carry out extensive trading activities in securities not covered by market abuse rules, and whose behaviour includes actions that would be market abuse in other contexts.

There are, broadly, two arguments relating to this issue:

- It is not for investment banks to determine ethics, but to obey the law.
- Practices that are illegal (and that some may consider unethical) in certain cases, may undermine confidence in capital markets and trading more widely. Based on this argument, such behaviour would be considered unethical from a utilitarian and deontological perspective in that it undermines orderly markets and potentially encourages disorderly markets.

Although the trust required to be reposed in markets by market participants is limited, there may be a greater than required level of trust placed on investment banks by many counterparties. Upholding market values outside of those markets would be ethical. Failing to do so might in some cases be unethical, especially where the proscribed market activity is both illegal and unethical (as opposed to solely being illegal).

The question over which approach – only following the letter of the law or applying the underlying spirit – is correct is also informed by an understanding of whether the ethical rights or duties of an investment bank take precedence. If an investment bank is simply another market participant without wider duties to the market, then there is less apparent reason why the investment bank cannot exploit all trading opportunities. However, it has become clear that political and public expectations of behaviour, which are part of our understanding of ethics, can affect the standing and value of investment banks (see Chapter 5 for a further discussion on this issue), and can imply ethical duties, especially where investment banks have increased ethical duties as a result of benefitting from Government intervention.

Market announcements and communications

Investment banks are often retained to assist clients with their communications and transactions involving their institutional shareholders, through ECM advisory activities, or corporate broking in the UK.

For an investment bank, communications with the market on behalf of a client is an area that can raise difficult ethical issues. The investment bank has a duty to assist its clients, and can be under pressure from a client to assist in raising their share price. Yet the way in which announcements are handled and information is announced to the market can affect the share price reaction to the news. Information can be presented in a positive way, but there is a line, not always clear, beyond which placing an overly positive slant on information can be misleading. In essence, providing information that, while strictly correct, is actively misleading, is in itself unethical, for two reasons: first, it undermines the markets themselves, and second, even while being strictly accurate, it is tantamount to lying.

While, from an ethical point of view, honesty in communications is essential and transparency is desirable, within a competitive market situation the issue is complicated by the need for confidentiality. The *de minimis* ethical position should therefore be to avoid dishonesty or deliberately withholding information in order to distort the truth.

Equity research

It is in an investment bank's interest for its equity research analysts to be seen as being influential in the market, as this assists in attracting both commission business (equity sales and trading) and also corporate business (primary and secondary issuance of securities).

An investment bank might use its trading capability in conjunction with analyst research in two principal ways: first, it might buy shares (through its market-making activities) in stocks covered by the research, in anticipation of market demand (a legitimate activity); and second, it might trade on the day the research is published in line with the recommendations, which could enhance any price movement triggered by the research.

When an equity analyst publishes a major piece of research, the investment bank has an interest in ensuring that the research is seen as affecting the market view of the value of the shares covered by the research. There are various ways in which an investment bank can effect this, for example by effective marketing across the bank's sales force to its entire client base. It is possible, and normally legitimate, for an investment bank's trading strategy through its market makers to support the research. Such support could potentially be viewed in some cases as market manipulation, but alternatively can be seen as the investment bank enabling its clients to trade. Ultimately, if the view is taken that markets are more or less efficient, it is unlikely that an investment bank would be able to profit from this type of support if the analysts' research were not genuinely incisive. The boundaries between this type of support and some of the examples of market abuse are not always clear-cut.

How exceptions affect ethics

There are exceptions to some proscribed activities, such as insider dealing and market abuse. These exceptions raise questions over the nature of the ethical objections to the practices concerned.

The specific exceptions or exemptions relating to takeovers and stabilisation helps us understand their nature and intent.

Under the UK's Takeover Code, it is permissible for a principal to acquire shares ahead of announcing a takeover offer. The difference between these activities and insider dealing is not only that these are legal, but also that they are part of a larger transaction which may depend on the exempted activities taking place.

Under European Commission regulation number 2273/2003,[5] exemptions from the market abuse regime are applicable under some circumstances for issuers of securities carrying out stabilisation or buy-back programmes. Stabilisation is a process enabling issuers of securities and their investment banks to trade in the market to hold up price levels in the wake of a new issue. Stabilisation is frequently necessary in order to successfully complete capital raisings, as in the initial period following the issue of securities prices can be volatile. Investors may be less willing to purchase new securities if they see a serious risk of prices reducing below the issue level shortly afterwards. However, if stabilisation is ethically acceptable to support the interest of specific issuers and investors, it raises questions over whether other very similar forms of such behaviour should be considered unethical.

In a similar way, exceptions to insider dealing rules suggest that insider dealing is unethical specifically in relation to market operations, but that this is based primarily on a utilitarian argument, and from other ethical perspectives insider dealing is not unethical. If insider dealing is allowed in certain circumstances, then it is difficult to consider it unethical from a "virtue" perspective. The position from a deontological perspective is less clear, with investment banks having a duty to support the markets they trade in: there is a risk that engaging in insider dealing undermines standards of market conduct and therefore confidence in markets.

The existence of and need for exemptions from market abuse rules in areas such as stabilisation raise the question of to what extent market abuse rules are ethical, in that they promote behaviour required to make markets work in a particular way and therefore are ethical from a utilitarian perspective, and to what extent the rules relate to behaviour that is ethical from the perspective of virtue.

> The existence of exemptions suggests that some proscribed market activities, including insider dealing, are not based on ethical rules that would stand the test of being "objective", and therefore cannot be regarded as ethical views from all ethical perspectives, notably from the perspective of "virtue".
>
> These are ethical rules from the utilitarian perspective, in that they help specific markets function. As discussed under insider dealing, it could nonetheless be unethical for such investment banks to engage in the types of behaviour listed above as market abuse specifically, in that investment banks benefit from orderly markets and there is therefore an ethical duty on them to generally uphold markets and market standards of conduct.

Off-market trading and the role of the CDO and CDS markets in the financial crisis

Some specific features of the financial crisis are apparently novel, notably the role of the CDO and CDS "markets". CDSs are instruments not historically traded on any recognised market, but nonetheless are now traded on a global scale. The scale of fraud relating to mortgage application and approval in the sub-prime mortgage market in the US is also different from problems in the recent past. There have been historical precedents of large-scale bubbles in unlisted securities – such as the notorious South Sea Bubble of 1720. However, such a widespread development of a massive market in unlisted securities in such a short time frame was a distinguishing feature of the sub-prime crisis. This in itself does not raise ethical concerns, but given the novelty of the products, the duty of care on institutions trading in or investing in such products should have been very high.

Trading off-market is not in itself unethical. However, investment banks may behave unethically if they adopt different standards to off-market activities from those which they apply on-market.

Speculation

During the financial crisis, some politicians, notably in Germany, criticised "speculators". Traditionally, a distinction has been drawn between activities considered "investment" and those considered "speculation".

The recent criticisms of "speculators" were not based on the traditional view of speculation (set out below), but on the belief that a particular type of trader or investor is able to inflict unjustified harm on issuers of securities (i.e., a company or a sovereign state).

To understand the concerns over speculative behaviour in the financial crisis, it is useful to look at the more traditional concept of speculation, seen as something akin to gambling, and to compare it with the idea of an actively destructive form of speculative investment.

Traditional views of speculation

There are a number of ways in which speculation has traditionally been distinguished from what we will refer to as "investment". First, based on research; second, based on control, or abuse; and third, based on the investment timescale, that is, how long an investment may be owned:

- Research: a distinction is sometimes drawn between investment and speculation where investment has been considered to be based on some form of research, and aimed at securing a return without risking the value of the principal amount invested. Conversely, speculation has been considered to be based on a lack of research. By implication, speculation is considered a form of "gambling" rather than investment, hence the term "casino capitalism".
- Control: alternatively, speculation can be considered to be investment in securities where only a minority holding is acquired and where there is, therefore, no real management control of an enterprise. This type of investment is prevalent in the modern economy, among pension funds, mutual funds and private investors, and in the context of modern markets is difficult to see this as unethical. Ethical concerns about the position of minority shareholders, including those who trade actively,

may, at least in part, be obviated by such investors exercising their share-holder rights (and duties) in terms of, for example, voting at company annual meetings (AGMs).

- Investment horizon: taking the traditional idea of a speculator, it is diffi-cult to make an ethical distinction between investment and speculation based primarily or exclusively on the length of time investors hold secu-rities, if in all other aspects their behaviour is similar. Investors with an indexing strategy may not carry out significant fundamental research on their investments, and may hold some stocks for limited time peri-ods (because they enter and then leave an index) but may not be typical "speculators".

From an ethical perspective, when the traditional view of speculation is examined, the more useful distinction from an ethical perspective is not between investment and "speculation", but specifically between investment and "gambling".

- The nature of "investment" is that it almost certainly involves some level of risk-taking, but can be based on detailed research and is fun-damentally supporting economic activity, even if only by providing liquidity to capital markets.
- The nature of gambling is that risk is understood, but returns are by definition subject to overwhelming random features that cannot be managed or controlled, and that are expected to give rise to an undeserved return (undeserved as relating to being based on economic activity).

In some ways, in stock markets, most equity investment is a form of spec-ulation, in that it involves taking risks (in Islamic finance, risk-taking is considered to be ethically necessary in an investment).

There is a major difference between short-term trading and "gambling", as in the latter case an unearned return is sought based on chance, rather than work or effort. Hedge funds or investment banks trading distressed securities are likely to carry out at least as much research as long-only investment managers, and significantly more than index funds, given the high levels of risk they take; it is therefore difficult to equate this type of activity to gambling.

This raises interesting questions about whether, for example, a pro-fessional poker player who bases their playing on an understanding of mathematical odds is therefore strictly a "gambler" (based on a narrow definition). Gambling is considered unethical for its general impact, in terms of damage to people who become addicted to it, and the collateral impact on their families. Ethical concerns regarding gambling can be advanced on a secular as well as a religious basis. Gambling – taking risks and seeking a reward without basing it on an "earned" return – would be considered unethical by the major religions.

With most investment in the capital markets – although any given security would be expected to show stochastic or random volatility and therefore has some of the features of gambling – in principle and over time market valuation should reflect fundamental value.

Speculation in the financial crisis

Concern over speculation in the financial crisis appears to be focused on activities that go beyond the normal definition of "speculation", and instead relate to a combination of abusive trading – attempting to destabilise a company or an issuer of securities – with very short-term trading.

The German Chancellor, Angela Merkel, has made a number of comments regarding speculation and short-selling, such as that: "We must succeed in putting an end to the speculators' game with sovereign states."[6] This type of criticism of the role of "speculators" in the financial crisis may be a combination of a political position, seeking an outside party or parties to blame, together with a real concern that some traders could actively attempt to bring about the insolvency of financial institutions or even sovereign states.

This suggests an actively destructive approach by speculative investors, very different to the traditional view of speculation as gambling or attempting to make an unearned or undeserved profit. Strategies actively aimed at causing economic harm (as opposed to profiting from an economic decline) are unethical, due to the damage they can cause.

Ethically, taking a negative view on the likely performance of a security and investing to profit if that view is correct, is not in itself problematic. The role of speculation in the financial crisis was probably overstated by some politicians. However, attempting to actively cause financial harm through an investment strategy would be unethical.

Types of activity considered "speculation", such as very short-term trading of distressed equities can be legitimate and ethical forms of investment. They would become unethical if they formed part of a strategy actively aimed at inflicting economic harm, for example by attempting to bring about the insolvency of an otherwise solvent institution.

Stock allocation and investment recommendations – The dotcom bubble

There were specific ethical problems associated with the dotcom bubble, many of which have been subject to detailed and highly public investigation by regulators and politicians. The dotcom crisis in 2001, following the 1999–2001 dotcom bubble, highlighted a series of specific ethical shortcomings among investment bankers, but with less devastating effect on the investment banking sector or on other parts of the economy than the financial crisis (largely as the dotcom sector was effectively unleveraged). It was followed by a series of legal and regulatory reviews and actions in relation to, among others:

- Allocation of "hot" Initial Public Offerings (IPOs) – stock being allocated to private trading accounts of clients or marketing prospects.
- False investment recommendations – analysts whose views on stocks differed from the advice given in their investment research.

These activities are clearly unethical, and went against accepted normal market practice at the time. In the case of hot-stock IPOs, this is because the job of the co-ordinating investment bank of an equity issue – which is to obtain both the best price and an orderly after-market – was prejudiced by investment banks placing equity with inappropriate investors. False or insincere investment recommendations, a major problem in the dotcom crash, were to some extent resolved by enforcing a strict separation between equity research and other parts of an investment bank, and by providing enhanced disclosure in equity research.

These ethical problems are akin to unauthorised trading, in that they are clearly unethical, rather than being ethically more complex, as with short-selling.

Short-selling

At the time the financial crisis was unfolding, short-selling was presented by some politicians and parts of the media as one of the major "abuses" of the financial crisis. It was blamed by some banks and Governments for destroying, or attempting to destroy, (quoted) banks. As such, it is in a different position from other practices, in that it was not illegal in most jurisdictions at the time, although it had previously been subject to some ethical concerns.

   The ethical position of short-selling is straightforward: it is not, in itself, unethical. Shorting can be broken down into two clear component actions: selling a share, and owing a share. To sell a share is not in itself unethical. To owe something is also not unethical. However, shorting as part of some other unethical activity, such as market manipulation or insider dealing, would normally be unethical from the perspective of both intention and consequences.

   The actual act of short-selling is no more than selling a share. It is difficult to consider this in itself as unethical. The driver for short-selling is to profit from share price movements. Profiting from a different investment view is a component of buying shares, as well as shorting, and is a well-understood fundamental basis of economic behaviour. It is true that short-selling can be abused: it can be used to move market prices for abusive reasons, for example in cases where an investor stands to profit from the insolvency of a company due to a short position (or holding credit default insurance such as CDS); it can be used to facilitate insider dealing; and it can be used to deliberately create distress in a company or for an investor. However, this is no more than the counterpart to the risk of the act of buying shares, which also is potentially subject to abuse (e.g., via insider dealing). As such, to postulate an objection to "short-selling" would be different in character from most ethical concerns regarding market practices.

   There is extensive evidence that short-selling leads to increased market liquidity, often viewed by economists and market practitioners as ethically beneficial. For example, it can assist in preventing investment "bubbles" from materialising. It is a sad fact that when poor investment decisions are made or when companies are poorly run, investors suffer. However, in this context, allowing market mechanisms to expose poor performance or management at an early stage can assist in preventing greater subsequent losses.

   Neither the FSA in the UK nor the SEC in the US, having reviewed the practice of short-selling, has considered it so vulnerable to abuse that this offsets the benefits of allowing the activity to continue.

   Shorting is often carried out as part of a "pairs trade". This means that an investor takes a view that company A is overvalued and company B is undervalued, and buys the same value of shares in company B as is sold in company A. This maintains a market neutral position, obviating risks to the investment position associated with general market movements at the same time as reducing the capital committed to the investment position. If the investor is correct, a high return can be achieved.

Short-selling is not something recently invented or characteristic only of financial markets. It has been commonplace in commodity – especially agricultural – markets for a long time.

The issue of short-selling can be separated into questions over selling a share and over being in a short position. On selling shares it is accepted that this activity is not in itself (absent some abusive intent) unethical. On being in a short position, take the following example: a farmer expecting to harvest 100 tonnes of grain sells 80 tonnes in advance of the harvest to pay for harvesting/new seed for the next season. Due to poor weather conditions (as can occur) only 70 tonnes is harvested. The farmer is then short 10 tonnes, which he has to make up by buying grain. For the period he is short of 10 tonnes of grain, could this be considered in some way unethical?

As neither (i) selling a share, nor (ii) being in a short position is in itself normally unethical, it is difficult to see the act of short-selling a share (or an index or a commodity) as intrinsically problematic from an ethical perspective, although this is not to say that shorting cannot be abusive for reasons already stated. It is likely that all major banks and investment banks participate in some of their activities either in short-selling or in facilitating short-selling.

Short-selling: Market evidence

Both the US and the UK implemented short-term bans on short-selling. Both bans were subsequently terminated.

In September 2008, short-selling was seen as a contributing factor to undesirable market volatility in the US and subsequently was prohibited in the US by the SEC. The SEC banned for three weeks short-selling on 799 financial stocks to boost investor confidence and stabilise those companies. In December 2008, SEC Chairman Christopher Cox said that the decision to impose the ban on the short-selling of financial company stocks was taken reluctantly, but that the view at the time, including that of Treasury Secretary Henry M. Paulson and Federal Reserve Chairman Ben S. Bernanke, was that "if we did not act and act at that instant, these financial institutions could fail as a result and there would be nothing left to save".[7] In 2009, Cox described the action as unproductive. At that time, the SEC's Office of Economic Analysis was still evaluating data from the temporary ban, with preliminary findings pointing to several unintended market consequences and side effects: "While the actual effects of this temporary action will not be fully understood for many more months, if not years," Cox said, "knowing what we know now, I believe on balance the Commission would not do it again."[8]

In September 2008, the FSA introduced emergency measures in relation to 32 stocks in UK financial sector companies due to the potential destabilising effects of short-selling in the extreme conditions prevailing and concerns about the potential for market abuse it posed. This effectively banned the active creation or increase of net short positions in the stocks of UK financial sector companies and required disclosure to the market of significant short positions in those stocks. The FSA introduced the measures without consultation as it was considered there was an urgent need to do so, but gave them a limited life as they were set to expire on 16 January 2009. Following a short consultation in January 2009 the FSA allowed the ban to expire but extended the Disclosure Obligation until 30 June 2009. In February 2009, the FSA published a Discussion Paper on short-selling. This examined the arguments for and against restrictions on short-selling. It proposed a disclosure requirement for the short-selling of all stocks, not just those of financial services companies, using an initial disclosure threshold of 0.5 per cent of issued share capital.[9]

The FSA conclusions in the February 2009 Discussion Paper included observing that bid-ask spreads for stocks where the ban was implemented rose considerably more than for the market as a whole. Rising spreads indicated that the market was working less efficiently and therefore the short-selling ban would penalise both buyers and sellers. Assessing the impact on market makers is harder, as they would have increased risk, with an increased opportunity to make or lose money.

> **Short-selling was blamed by some politicians and media commentators for inflicting damage during the financial crisis. This was not substantiated by subsequent enquiries. While it is capable of being abused, short-selling is not in itself unethical, but can be part of a reasonable and ethical investment strategy.**

Ethical implications for investment banks

- The ethical implications of practices criticised during the financial crisis are not uniform.
- It is unethical to manipulate information, such as presentations to rating agencies, to give a false impression.

- Mis-selling presents particular ethical issues, both in securities and in M&A. In both cases, there can be incentives for lying or misleading. Ethically, it is important to look at both the intention and the outcome of the situation.
- Insider dealing raises specific ethical issues: it is not unambiguously unethical, and is not uniformly illegal. Breaching confidentiality, which is normally concomitant with insider dealing, is unethical. Overall, in practice, it is difficult to see how an investment bank could ethically support insider dealing even where it is legal.
- Market abuse covers a range of practices that are unethical, and in some cases illegal. Part of the reason why such practices are unethical is because of the public and political expectation of a high standard of behaviour.
- Speculation and short-selling, although heavily criticised, do not appear to be unethical *per se*, as long as they are not part of another abusive practice.

Chapter summary

- Political and public expectations of behaviour, which are part of our understanding of ethics, can affect the standing and value of investment banks. Some political criticism of practices such as "speculation" may be motivated by the desire to shift criticism away from the political arena, rather than accurately portraying investment banking behaviour.
- There is an ethical question over how far it is appropriate to "manage" a credit rating in order to get a desired outcome, both as a principal, and as an adviser. Ultimately, it is unethical to be complicit in a lie.
- The type of mis-selling seen where products, which have been understood by an investment bank to be flawed in some way, have been sold, highlights problems with a bank's potential conflicts of interest.
- Mis-selling is also possible in an M&A sales process. Lying in a sales process is unethical. Deliberately misleading can be more complicated, but would also be considered unethical.
- There are lending practices that may be unethical, including those associated with encouraging a debtor to incur greater indebtedness than is likely to be able to be serviced in order to profit from the situation.
- Trading and making losses is not unethical in itself. Trading without authorisation, or where management has given only "informal" authorisation, would be unethical.

- Market manipulation and market abuse cover a range of activities, which are illegal in some jurisdictions and in regard to some securities. These activities are unethical in that they undermine the confidence in and operation of markets. However, some of the practices proscribed in trading and marketing securities would be considered common practice in other sectors of the economy.
- Off-market trading is not unethical, but trading should be informed by ethical considerations.
- False or insincere investment recommendations, although partly resolved by enforcing a strict separation between equity research and other parts of an investment bank, are unethical.
- Speculation is considered a form of "gambling" rather than investment, hence the term "casino capitalism". It is difficult to see the type of investment strategy undertaken by investment banks as speculative in this sense. Types of activity considered "speculation", such as very short-term trading of distressed equities can be legitimate and ethical forms of investment. They would become unethical if they formed part of a strategy actively aimed at inflicting economic harm, for example by attempting to bring about the insolvency of an otherwise solvent institution.
- Short-selling is not unethical in itself, but is unethical where it is part of an unethical strategy.
- Many of the market practices common among investment banks and other investors, and many of the practices criticised during the financial crisis, are ethically ambiguous. Both the intention and consequences need to be examined in order to assess the practices' ethical value.

How should ethical issues be considered in dealing with market practices that are legal but may be unethical? Can you describe the potential ethical benefits and harm that arise from the type of trading activity described as "speculation"?

7
Ethical Issues – Clients

It was argued in Chapter 6 that duties towards stakeholders should take precedence over a firm's rights. Central to this, therefore, is how an investment bank treats its clients. We would highlight three broad areas of concern:

- conflicts of interest;
- the duty of care to a client;
- more specifically, truth and honesty in dealing with clients.

There is much ethical analysis of key concepts relating to these issues, notably **promises** and **truth**, and also much analysis of how closely, from an ethical perspective, misleading relates to lying. An understanding of these from an ethical perspective is important to be able to understand how they relate to ethics in investment banking, and to guide behaviour.

Promises

Market behaviour centres on keeping promises, and believing that others will do so. There is a constant reminder of this with the statement on UK banknotes: "I promise to pay the bearer on demand the sum of ... " Markets only work because participants believe their contracts will be honoured. Keeping promises is archetypal good ethical behaviour as it engenders trust. US dollar bills state "In God we trust" – the implication being that trust is of fundamental importance. Markets can therefore be considered to encourage some forms of ethical behaviour, albeit these are very specific and limited in extent.

The importance of promises, although central to market activity, is not central to other areas of investment banking. Investment banks that behave according to normal market principles in some areas, will typically act using different standards in other areas. Applying different ethical standards in different areas of a business is not something that can be easily reconciled (see the market abuse section for a more detailed discussion).

Truth and honesty

There are a number of ethical dilemmas facing investment banking relating to truth, lying and misleading.

For those in a corporate finance or M&A department, in a sales process there are often times where the line between describing a business for sale effectively (which is *per se* ethical) and untruthfully (which is *per se* unethical) can become blurred.

For capital markets, there are similar issues with supporting corporate clients, whether in an IPO, a secondary issue or the sale of securities. In equity research, this issue is well understood, and equity analysts now have clear requirements for independence.

Is misleading different from lying?

There is the associated issue of being strictly truthful but knowingly misleading. Is this in itself any different from lying?

While few investment bankers will offer outright lies, many will speak extremely precisely, in a way designed to give a certain impression, which may be misleading.

Is there an ethical difference between misleading and lying? If the impression at the end of the process is the same, and the words are chosen so carefully that they are very unlikely to be decoded correctly, then **misleading is ethically similar to lying** as it seeks to influence an outcome through the use of misinformation. This is an area where the ethical implications of an action may be different from the legal implications.

Where should the line be drawn?

For an investment bank, it can be difficult to know where to differentiate between a clear "marketing" claim, which might be a justifiable statement, and one that is actively misleading. This is especially the case in a "beauty parade", where other investment banks might be expected to put their case in the most compelling manner possible.

The context of much of an investment banker's external discussion is some form of negotiation or competition, whether in the capital markets or as an adviser. For example, an equity analyst will be inclined to defend a research opinion, rather than state both sides of an investment case. Alternatively, an adviser will be talking to a putative acquirer or seller of a business. In both these cases, the investment banker's typical position will be that determined by the need to negotiate. That is, to take a significantly more clear-cut position than would be required in normal discourse. Understood in this context, careful use of wording and taking strong (or even extreme) positions can be ethically justifiable, up to an ill-defined point where ethical judgement needs to be used. As an example, an equity analyst will often be of more use to an investor if they have a strong opinion on a stock, as this can, in the context of a market where multiple research views are available, serve to illuminate additional aspects of a company's performance or value.

It is not reasonable to suggest that a pitch document or sales script should be verified in the same way as a prospectus or information memorandum. However, there are some basic precepts that can usefully be applied:

- Wording used should not be actively misleading or deliberately untrue.
- There is frequent criticism by clients of investment banks who practice "bait and switch" (see below). A team presented at a pitch should be genuinely expected (at the time – in transactions situations can change rapidly) to execute the transaction, or the pitch should clearly disclose the team that is to execute the transaction.
- Special care should be taken in describing conflicts of interest (as opposed to explaining why such conflicts do not exist or are not relevant).
- The duty of care shown to a client should always be taken seriously, and the resources committed to the client should be made available.

Bait and switch

The client of an investment bank appoints the investment bank for a combination of reasons, including their expertise, resources and market presence. The investment bank is almost certainly relatively expensive simply because of its level of resource (e.g., an accountancy firm is likely to prove less costly on an hourly basis). The senior banker or bankers at a pitch will discuss their relationships with potential buyers, sellers or investors. It can be galling to the client if the senior banker, once appointed, effectively disappears once a mandate is awarded.

An investment bank is both an institution and the sum of its key individuals. However, there is always a specific core team who is responsible for delivering that expertise in any transaction. An investment bank, when pitching to a client, may claim a level of knowledge or relationship that may be strictly accurately presented, but not genuinely available. In some cases, an investment bank may accurately state a firm's expertise without revealing that the person in whom some specific knowledge or a specific relationship rested has left the firm or moved to another role. This can give a deliberately misleading picture of an investment bank's capabilities. A similar issue can arise where an investment banker is discussing their relationships with a broad universe of counterparties, in which case it can be very tempting to overstate (sometimes very substantially) the depth of some of these relationships.

Notably, in an advisory assignment, a client will expect the senior banker who comes into a pitch to know where the counterparties are coming from and to intercede with the direct decision-maker. However, because of the way investment banks are structured, with work often being pushed down to junior investment bankers, it can be the case that the investment bank's added-value turns out to be some relatively modest additional resource, which needs to be actively managed by the client due to the relative inexperience of the bankers concerned.

It can appear to a client that an investment bank puts more attention and resources – especially at a senior level – into winning a new client or a mandate than in maintaining a relationship.

Issuing securities

As discussed above, one of the most important ethical failures leading to the financial crisis was the mis-selling of securities.

An investment bank will carry out its activities in marketing securities in two main ways:

- In "secondary market" sales and trading of securities, which will be based in part on offering prices to buy or sell stock ("market-making"), in part on meeting client demand and in part on marketing the views of the investment bank's research department.
- In "primary market" sales and trading, where the investment bank will be selling new securities.

It is in the context of primary market issuance of securities that the question of whether an investment bank believes in its product is most relevant. A prospectus for a primary issue will be published not by the issuer, but by the investment bank(s) sponsoring the issue. Internally within an investment bank, the question of whether it should support a particular primary issue is governed by two main factors: the fees associated with the issue, and whether the securities can be effectively placed or sold in the market. Investment banks might not ask whether they "believe" in a security other than in the context of whether it can be successfully sold, unless there are particular reasons to do so, for example where the investment bank might be expected to hold a meaningful amount of the securities following the issue. However, the issue of "belief" in a security, company or offering, at least implicitly if not explicitly includes consideration of the fundamental value of the offering.

It might be disadvantageous for investment banks to turn down participation in offerings that they are able to place in the market due to concerns over "belief" or fundamental value. Given the size of fees associated with primary issues, for investment banks to routinely not participate in offerings that can be placed in the market would be financially difficult. If such issues are successfully placed, then the investment bank that carries out the placing will have both better profitability and a better track record. The profitability can be used to hire the best-placed salesmen, traders and analysts to carry out further deals, and the track record can be used to attract new clients. Consequently, if there is market demand for securities, it can be highly detrimental to the market position of an investment bank to apply a restrictive approach to which securities will be sold.

Investment banks do look carefully at analyses of how different investment banks' new issues perform in the market – and some include such analysis in their marketing materials – as this can be a differentiating factor in winning business. This gives an incentive to apply some care in accepting mandates, but at least as relevantly may give an incentive to price new issues realistically.

Should investment banks decide whether to raise capital for a client based on a "belief" in the fundamental value of the company rather than on an understanding of market demand? From an ethical perspective, ideally this would be the case. However, in practice this is problematic. Investment banks would not necessarily be correct in their valuations (the track record of equity analysts suggests that stock recommendations can be inaccurate); different individuals in an investment bank might well have different views on value; and other market participants might not wish investment banks to reach judgements on value, which investors will see as their prerogative.

Although this suggests that it would be difficult for investment banks to market only those securities where they "believe" in the long-term value proposition, this is not to say that investment banks do not have an ethical duty not to sell securities that they believe will fail. The ethical duty on an investment bank may not require "belief" (in part, as this concept can be subjective) in the securities it sells, but there remains a duty to ensure that sufficient due diligence is completed to be able to genuinely justify or support their valuation. It is clearly unethical for an investment bank to market securities that it issues as a principal when it believes that such securities will fail.

Duty of care

An investment bank will have a duty of care to its clients. Given the range of different activities carried out within an investment bank, the nature of relationships with clients and of the duty of care will vary. At the stage when an investment bank agrees to take on a client, it has a duty to protect the client's interests. This implies that the bank will act in a client's interest in executing a transaction; will seek to give honest advice (honest in the sense of furthering a client's interest, as well as being truthful); and will utilise its resources (at least to the extent indicated by the investment bank prior to appointment) in furthering the client's interest.

However, given the wide range of services provided, what happens to the duty of care to one client while the investment bank is acting for another? This is also relevant when the investment bank is itself acting as a principal in a transaction.

As discussed in Chapter 6, the capital markets department of an investment bank may have simultaneously different relationships with the same client. Being clear at all time as to what this implies for the investment bank's duty of care may be complicated, but it is essential if an investment bank is to carry out all its activities to high ethical standards.

This is typically complex for institutional salesmen, for whom an institutional investor is sometimes a commission-paying client and sometimes a "customer" purchasing securities from the investment bank, perhaps even in the same conversation. Given this complexity, the investment bank has an increased duty to behave honestly and not present false or misleading information.

Conflicts of interest

Perhaps the most ubiquitous ethical problem facing investment banks is how to handle conflicts of interest. Conflicts of interest can pose real ethical – as well as practical – dilemmas in terms of relationships with clients.

Being party to information that can be used against a client's best interest, and where there is an incentive to do so, raises serious questions of fairness, honesty and trust; while being pulled in two directions when making a business decision is generally problematic.

Typical conflicts of interest would be:

- Acting for an issuer of securities, where securities are placed with institutional investors who are, in other contexts, clients of the firm (discussed in Chapter 6).
- Acting for two clients in the same transaction, for example offering finance to two clients to support the same transaction.
- Trading in a company's securities while acting on an advisory or capital raising assignment.
- Advising a company on a transaction while seeking to provide finance to support the transaction.

In the main, these involve an investment bank acting for different parties who have an involvement in the same transaction. These can also apply to situations where fees related to financing could influence the objectivity of the advice.

An integrated investment bank may serve many clients with an interest in the same transaction, for example when issuing securities. The clearest problem of conflicts comes when an investment bank seeks to act for two clients in the same transaction without disclosing that it is doing so. There remains a question, even where such activities are disclosed, as to whether it is ethical to do so.

It is inevitable that conflicts of interest will arise in an integrated investment bank. All investment banks have policies to deal with such situations – the basic approach to take to such conflicts is to follow the policy. However, the incentive for an investment bank is to maximise its revenue. Consequently, there is always pressure to proceed with a mandate if a conflict of interest can be managed. In many cases, the appropriate resolution to a conflict is to disclose the conflict and sometimes to seek written consent from clients. In cases where such disclosure is not possible (e.g., where the conflict concerns relationships with two rival firms who cannot be made aware of each others' activities) it is difficult to see how the investment bank can continue to act for all parties concerned with integrity.

As part of its marketing for investment banking mandates, the investment bank will typically indicate that it will put all necessary resources at a client's disposal. This is simply not possible where there is a direct conflict of interest with another party.

Investment banks have procedures in place for dealing with conflicts. These can be formal or ad hoc as necessary. However, the incentive for an investment bank is very much to have conflicts: there is an aphorism in investment banking that "conflicts of interest = revenue" (which is generally correct, on a number of levels). Therefore, investment banks will seek to *manage* such conflicts of interest, rather than to avoid them.

Conflicts of interest can give rise to significant concerns. On 14 February 2011, a Delaware court criticised the behaviour of Barclays Capital in its role advising Del Monte Foods Co. on a sale, when it was also acting as a debt provider to the company's proposed buyer. Notably, the lawsuit was brought by shareholders (Barclays was not at the time a defendant, and rejected the criticism). This highlights the perceived conflict of interest of advising on a sale and financing a buyer.

Despite the conflict of interest created by a situation where an adviser to a seller also finances (or advises) a buyer, and incentives created by the fact that financing fees are often significantly higher compared with the advisory fees on a sale, there remains a cogent argument that it is helpful to a seller for its adviser to be prepared to finance a buyer of a business. This is because the sell-side adviser may become more comfortable with the credit risk in the business being sold, and therefore offer more advantageous financing, which would aid both seller and buyer. This argument, although cogent, is not always compelling, for two main reasons: first, the due diligence process ought to be orchestrated by the sell-side adviser to give sufficient information for other providers of finance to put an equivalent financing package together; and second, the incentives created by the financing fees can undermine the sell-side adviser's duty to their (sell-side) client. The argument for a sell-side adviser to also offer financing to buyers is most cogent in a situation where the provision of debt finance is problematic.

Corporate finance

For a corporate financier, two common sources of conflict are having an advisory relationship with both the buyer and the seller in a transaction and seeking to provide finance to an advisory client or to a counterparty.

Having an advisory relationship with both buyer and seller can be beneficial to both, but can also be seen as a conflict. From an ethical standpoint, as long as a client understands the multiple relationships that an investment bank may have, it is difficult to see such relationships as presenting a conflict.

However, it is difficult to see how one organisation can represent both the buyer and seller in the same transaction. This is particularly the case where there are success fees relating to the transaction. For example, there are clear incentives for a sell-side adviser to maximise fees by achieving a sale at the best possible price, but this potentially creates a conflict if the same investment bank is also advising a buyer – especially where there is a weak field of buyers.

The issues behind providing both advice and finance are complex: many clients will use an integrated investment bank (at least in part) because of its ability to finance a transaction. At the same time, given the significantly higher fees associated with financing in comparison to advice, the provision of financing makes it, in practice, difficult to always give objective advice. As with other conflicts of interest, the key responsibility of the banker concerned is to be transparent to the client.

For the heads of department, or a MD responsible for a client, there is likely to be real pressure to maximise revenue from a transaction, and this can lead to a focus on achieving the (higher) financing fees at the possible expense of giving objective advice. Sometimes this can result in bad advice being given, at other times this does not present a real conflict. Generally, it is in an investment bank's best interest to give honest advice: bad advice may lead to a bank having financing exposure to a defaulting transaction. In practice a client will perceive whether an adviser is being straightforward in their advice, and to be less than straightforward can prejudice the client relationship and therefore also have negative consequences for revenue for the investment bank. In addition, a client's motivation in carrying out a transaction may not be shared with their adviser, and there are certainly cases where an adviser's negative view on a transaction is a hindrance to a client executing a transaction.

The trusted adviser

For advisers, the question of trust can be a major issue where investment banks are hired for the capabilities and knowledge of specific, relatively small teams of people. This can be a real area of difficulty: investment bankers using knowledge gained from acting for one client can assist in marketing to a competitor or in advising an acquirer of the client. In practice, most corporations realise that there are limits as to what should be disclosed to investment bankers, due to the likelihood of their investment bankers also working for competitors or acquirers. In the UK, a company's nominated financial adviser is prevented from acting on an acquisition of the company by the Takeover Panel. However, this is normally academic, as a nominated adviser would expect to act only for the company being acquired in such a situation. Where this rule has not been followed, the company can ask the Takeover Panel to require the adviser to step down from advising the acquirer.

There are two particular sets of circumstances where a conflict of interest can arise in this regard:

- Where a bank has two major clients who are not normally in competition, but where one attempts to acquire the other. Although an investment bank could in theory choose to step down from advising both the sides, in practice this is very unlikely to be the first choice.
- Where an investment bank has a specialist group, focused, for example, on a specific industry, where the role of the bankers necessitates close relationships and detailed knowledge of all major players in a sector.

Investment banks have detailed processes in place to resolve such conflicts. The day-to-day marketing activity of investment bankers can involve trading significant amounts of information between clients – it is unclear to what extent this is actually productive and to what extent counterproductive, given the requirement to be trusted by clients to execute most mandates. An exception to this may be "sell-side" mandates, where an investment bank advising on the sale of a subsidiary may benefit from demonstrating its ability to understand a range of competitors, who will form a natural buyer universe.

There is a significant difference between being wrong – presenting an incorrect conclusion – and presenting a conclusion that is not merited by the facts as they are understood. The incentive is for investment bankers to facilitate transactions – it is transactions that typically create the scope for investment banks to earn fees. This incentive is sufficiently strong that investment bankers are likely to have a bias against advising clients not to enter into transactions. This does not mean that investment bankers do not advise against deals, but it is a simple fact that the incentive is for investment bankers to normally encourage a transaction.

Capital markets

In capital markets, conflicts of interest typically relate to complex circumstances where a salesman, trader or analyst may deal with the same institutional investor from different perspectives. For example, the investor may be a commission-paying client in some cases, but may also be a buyer of securities when the investment bank is acting as a principal. In these cases, it is of paramount importance for the investment banker to first understand the conflict, and the duties of care involved, and, second, to be confident that these are understood by the client. In practice, on many occasions, this should not change the investment banker's behaviour.

There are also conflicts in capital markets' activities similar to those seen in corporate finance where pitching for business. In these cases, the issues are similar to those for corporate finance.

Pre-IPO financing/private equity

A further source of conflict can arise if an investment bank seeks to invest equity itself. As an example, if a client asks an investment bank to carry out an IPO, but the investment bank instead suggests making an investment itself – from which it seeks high returns – even though this would be followed at a later date by an IPO. This can be in a client's best interest, but on occasion it can also be advantageous to the investment bank, giving rise to a potential conflict of interest. In practice, many investment banks do not invest on this type of basis, so such conflicts are relatively uncommon.

Practical issues

In practice, there are some specific circumstances in which an investment bank may face particular pressure to behave unethically. These can be found, in particular, in pitching (or marketing in general), relationships with competitors, sell-side advisory assignments, and in various aspects of equity research. Particular concerns in these areas are set out below (the issue of conflicts within capital markets has been considered above).

Pitching

The archetypal set piece of investment banking, whether M&A, capital markets or corporate finance, is the beauty parade: teams from different investment banks are interviewed by a client in order for one firm to be appointed to an often remunerative and prestigious assignment. All the investment banks will have put substantial resource into preparing for the pitch. In many cases, only one investment bank will succeed, but the winner will be rewarded with very attractive fees. An exception to this is securities issuance, where a "syndicate" comprising a number of investment banks may be appointed, albeit (typically) one investment bank will be appointed as bookrunner, and earn the major share of available fees.

In a pitch, an investment bank will set out its credentials and its advice in the most favourable way possible. There can be a fine line between presenting this in an honest but exaggerated way and presenting it falsely. For example, an investment bank may claim to have advised on another relevant transaction, but their advice may in reality have been very limited in scope. Inevitably, some elements of pitching are prone to exaggeration, but in some cases investment banks go further and pitches can contain actively misleading information. Areas where an investment banking pitch may be exaggerated would include the range of relationships with interested buyers or sellers of a business or shares; the amount of work carried out on similar engagements; the specific experience of the proposed team; and notoriously the personal time commitment of the senior bankers concerned.

As with a sell-side assignment, it can reasonably be assumed that the buyer of investment banking services will know that investment bank(er)s tend to exaggerate. This does not, however, make an unethical act less unethical.

Sell-side advisers

In practice, a client expects an investment banker to deliver a transaction (to complete it successfully), whether raising capital, or buying, selling or restructuring a business or securities. In the case of a sell-side engagement, this involves (i) achieving a sale, and (ii) doing so at the highest price possible. It would be very unusual for a client to insist on – or want – their investment banking adviser to be scrupulously honest. Given the known tendency of investment bankers in this situation to at least exaggerate, if not actively mislead or lie, buyers will typically discount what they are told by sell-side advisers.

Sometimes an investment banker will mislead potential buyers over the description of a business for sale – this should be noticed during due diligence by the buyer. It is more common and more productive to provide misleading information on the progress of the sale. This can involve giving a misleading impression regarding the number of buyers or the level of price being offered by other buyers.

There are some established tactics used by sell-side advisers that focus on giving away as little information as possible. This can be effective, but it depends on how attractive the subject is.

In the end, a successful sell-side adviser will be one who delivers successful sales at high prices. An adviser who is both credible and also able to mislead without being spotted will be more likely to be successful than one who is scrupulously honest. In addition, in a private sales process, the type of lie being told has little real risk of being discovered.

This is an area where it is easy to see the ethical problem, but difficult to see the likely adverse result. Sell-side advice is a difficult area for investment bankers. Risk-weighted fees are highly attractive, but there is more scope for gaining advantage by lying than in other areas of transaction execution.

The 2010 court case in New York between Terra Firma Capital Partners and Citigroup showed the risks associated with sell-side advice (the case was won by Citi). This case concerned both the question of whether a sell-side adviser gave false information, and also exposed issues of possible conflicts of interest. Terra Firma alleged that a Citi banker gave Terra Firma incorrect information regarding the auction of EMI, suggesting a price level that Terra Firma needed to exceed to buy the company, leading Terra Firma to make an excessive bid for EMI. Terra Firma sought over $8 billion in damages. The case was complicated by the complexity of Citi's position: Citi was an adviser to EMI and earned advisory fees of £6 million. Citi was also a lender to Terra Firma and earned over £86 million in financing fees. Managing a conflict between advising the seller of a business and financing a buyer raises significant problems, given the size of fee that can be achieved from cumulative success, and the level of unrecovered costs in the event of failure. The incentives for an investment bank and the investment bankers concerned to succeed generate high levels of pressure, which must encourage unethical behaviour. Managing such situations to retain high ethical standards requires both management commitment and clear inculcation of ethical standards.

There are difficulties for an integrated investment bank to manage conflicts associated with advising the seller of a business and financing the buyer. Nonetheless, this practice has become relatively common – including offering "stapled financing" as part of a sell-side transaction. That is, offering a financing package available to whoever buys a business. The argument for an existing adviser providing finance is that it assists clients, as the investment bank is institutionally more comfortable with the credit quality of the asset. At the same time, given the size of the financing fees, it may put increased pressure on the sell-side adviser to deliver a particular deal.

Looking generally at sell-side situations, a sell-side adviser has a clear informational advantage over a buyer. In an auction, pricing will generally be significantly better if there are two or more well-capitalised buyers willing to buy the business being sold. Where this is not the case, part of the art of the sell-side adviser is to find a way to achieve a price that is equivalent to the level which would result from a competitive auction. One way to do this involves making the process look as though there is "price tension" between buyers. This could involve providing only scant information, so the potential buyer has no real knowledge of how competitive the process is or is not. Another way would be to use the position of other interested parties very selectively even if their interest is low or they are not credible (e.g., poorly financed). This would avoid lying, but present the position in the most favourable way possible. A third way is to "bluff", or put more simply, to lie. Lying in these circumstances is potentially damaging for the investment bank, but can be very effective in achieving the "right" result from an auction. Typically, investment banks receive an incentivised fee on the sale of a business – the higher the price they achieve, the higher their fee.

Relationships with competitors

With large fees – and compensation – payable to the investment bank and investment bankers mandated on a transaction, and potentially no fees payable to any bank not mandated, there is intense rivalry between investment banks. This level of competition can be healthy, encouraging innovation, high standards and good customer service. At the same time, it can have its dark side: unfair criticism by one investment bank or investment banker of another to a client can be defamatory.

Such criticism is often ignored by clients, and can be counterproductive. At the same time, personal criticisms aimed at investment bankers can sometimes stick and damage reputations, even if unfair.

Equity research

Following substantial regulatory reform in the wake of the dotcom crash, equity research was not a major source of ethical concern during the financial crisis, although it was a source of significant regulatory and legal concern during and after the dotcom crash. In 2003, ten major investment banks in the US agreed a "Global Settlement" to pay compensation and fines of $1.4 billion to settle cases brought by a number of regulators. Central to the issues raised by this case was the level of bias and conflicts of interest in investment research and advice. Subsequent to this case and the dotcom crash, there have been major changes to the way in which research is produced.

High-profile conflicts of interest included cases of equity analysts publishing research opinions that were contradicted by their own privately held views, and were influenced by pressure from clients of the investment bank and by investment bankers from advisory departments. Such conflicts are now less common, given tighter legislation and regulation protecting the integrity of analyst research.

Pressure was applied to analysts by investment bankers in advisory departments (such as equity capital markets) to maintain positive recommendations and high valuations on the shares of corporate clients and prospective clients of the investment bank. An equity analyst could be incentivised and instructed to write positive research. This in some cases led to research that was very flawed. Following reforms to securities regulation in the wake of the dotcom crash, equity research is now required to be separate from advisory activities. Equity analysts are protected from pressure from the investment bank: research is now required to be physically separate from investment banking, research analysts require approval from compliance departments in order to have meetings with investment bankers from advisory departments and analyst remuneration cannot be linked to investment banking transactions.

In addition to measures taken to ensure that undue influence is not applied to analysts, analysts are also required to disclose any information relevant to conflicts of interest, such as personal holdings in securities and any relevant corporate relationships of the investment bank.

While issues surrounding conflicts of interest are no longer major, research analysts still face ethical issues relating to their duty of care and relating to "truth" – levels of honesty in dealing with clients, and competence. In this case, the issues are likely to relate to:

- Identifying who has carried out the research. Many research teams have a high-profile lead analyst, and other less well-recognised junior analysts. The lead analyst will be required to spend significant amounts of time marketing as opposed to researching, but their name will be associated with any research that is published.
- How much analysis or primary research analysts have undertaken (this is also an issue faced by advisers). In reality, some analysts may still take a "black box" approach to research, publishing mainly the results of valuation exercises, without all the background analysis. This leaves significant scope to offer misleading commentary as to the extent and depth of the analysis underlying a conclusion.
- The strength of conviction behind a recommendation to purchase or sell a share.

These issues all affect the underlying quality of the research. Equity research is not simply about researching investment opportunities, but is also concerned with marketing a research product. The overall market reputation of an analyst can, in the short term, be as important as the nature of the published research. In the longer term, the quality of the research, including the timing and accuracy of recommendations, should be a significant element in an analyst's reputation.

There are also ethical concerns regarding personal account holdings of equity analysts. Some institutional investors actively favour analysts holding stocks that they recommend. Where personal holdings run counter to recommendations, this can raise questions regarding both ethics and credibility. In practice, this is less likely to be the case for a "buy" recommendation than for a "sell" recommendation.

The relationship between ethics and competence is an ongoing issue in equity research, and one that is relevant to the senior management of an investment bank, including the heads of research departments. Research analysts are unable to properly carry out their research if they are not sufficiently well trained, and there is both a professional/commercial need and an ethical requirement for research to be genuinely incisive.

Fees

Investment banking fees can be significant sums of money, and can result in investment bankers being paid a high multiple of average earnings. It is of great importance that investment bankers understand that the position they are in places them in a biased position, with possible incentives to behave unethically towards their clients.

How fees are determined should not only reflect market conditions and what is a fair return for banking services, but also the duty of care towards customers, which includes quality of service. So in setting fees a balance should be struck between profit, the cost of banking services and market forces.

Levels of investment banking fees do not typically give rise to ethical concerns, because:

- The level of fees typically paid by clients is a very small percentage of the size of a transaction and unlikely to determine a client's decision on whether or not a transaction is undertaken.

- Investment banking is a relatively competitive industry, and an individual investment bank is unlikely to be able to demand fees in the absence of competitive pressure.

There are, however, occasions when fees might present specific ethical concerns. It is not possible to set these out in totality, but examples would include:

- Situations where the level of fee is such that a client regrets entering a transaction. This might be the case, for example, in a relatively unsuccessful transaction where the minimum fee is a relatively high proportion of transaction value (such as an equity issue for which there is little demand).
- Situations where the fee is agreed by a client not properly interested in negotiating the fee. This might be the case in a restructuring, where a fee might be agreed with a class of investor whose returns from the transaction would not materially be affected by fee levels.
- Situations where the client is relatively naive, and agrees a fee without fully understanding market norms; for example, where a client has recently promoted a new CEO who is not familiar with such transactions.

In the latter two cases, the investment bank should consider the ethics of the fees being sought, and not simply seek to optimise its own income.

Investment banking fees do not simply follow a prescribed pattern. In some areas fees are relatively competitive, in others services may only be offered by a small number of specialist firms, and fees reflect the relative lack of competition.

There are a number of different types of fee paid to an investment bank for services, each of which is subject to different influences:

- Commission paid by institutions trading securities;
- Commission paid by an issuer of securities, which would typically be significantly higher than that paid for simple securities trading; and
- Advisory fees, such as those paid in an acquisition.

Of these, commissions are generally payable on reasonably well-understood market levels, although there is a significant scope for negotiation on the issue of new securities. Advisory fees can be highly variable, and it is not uncommon for the advisers on either side of a transaction to be paid on two very different bases.

Investment banking fees do not follow obvious relationships to time and effort in individual engagements. However, in most cases significant fees are only payable in the event of a transaction. Investment banks need to cover their costs for all their activities from the successful mandates only. Some potential users of investment banking services seek, where possible, to internalise such services in order to reduce their costs. Others may seek to be seen as good (i.e., high) payers of investment banking fees, with the aim of being seen as a preferred client and therefore gaining preferred access to capital or services. In some cases, an investment bank may not only receive a cash fee, but also receive securities in the client company (normally warrants or options). This is more likely to be the case with smaller companies.

Within an investment bank, the pressure on bankers responsible for a client or engagement is always to agree the highest possible fee. As discussed above, such fees are difficult to directly attribute to specific work, in the form of hours worked on an individual transaction. In order to distribute securities, an investment bank needs to have the market presence associated with significant infrastructure, such as research, sales and trading, as well as logistical capabilities. Fees paid for securities issuance therefore need to reflect a very long-term investment. This can also be the case, but to a markedly lesser extent, with most advisory transactions, where it is more likely that a small number of identifiable individuals are responsible for the key aspects of an engagement.

Where fees are negotiable, is it ethical to aim to achieve the highest possible fee from a client? The (at least) implicit assumption in an investment bank is that clients are able to manage their own affairs. It is also arguable that at the stage of a negotiation over fees, the investment bank is not yet retained and therefore does not have a duty of care to the client. There is a clear difference between charging the high end of an observable market rate for services, and charging outside market norms. However, it must also be noted that some specific clients (including Governments) seek to pay fees below market norms. It is open to investment banks not to accept such terms. However, many choose to do so due to the prestige of certain clients and mandates. Such an approach might make it necessary for an investment bank to achieve higher fees from other clients, or to change their cost base by reducing remuneration.

There are cases where investment banks achieve very high fees: these are normally where there is an incentive mechanism in place to reward an investment bank for exceeding a client's perspective. Under such circumstances, a client would have wanted such incentives to work, and it is difficult to see how high rewards are unethical if they are transparent and the fee-paying client fully understands the fee structure when it is agreed.

An investment banker may have a conflict of interest in relation to fees where a client could be advised or assisted with funding a transaction (or its normal activities). The level of fee associated with raising different forms of capital can vary substantially, and the incentive for the investment banker is normally to maximise fee income. Fees are generally expressed as a percentage of the capital raised, and vary from below 1 per cent for investment grade bonds, to around 2–3 per cent for equity and up to 5–7 percent for junior (junk) debt or mezzanine finance (these numbers are highly approximate – actual fee levels are highly variable depending on the issuer, and on the state of the market at the time of the capital raising).

For an adviser to a company, financing fees can significantly exceed M&A fees. For example, an adviser might stand to earn a fee of $5 million for advising on a $1 billion acquisition. If the acquisition were funded in part with debt, a $100 million junior debt tranche on its own could double the fees that the investment bank receives. Given that an investment bank might typically not retain a holding in the financing (although practices vary), the fee is paid for structuring and selling the financing, not for holding it for any period of time. For financing an entire $1 billion with debt, assuming an 80:20 mix of senior and junior debt for an investment grade company, fees could, for example, total over $8 million for senior debt and over $10 million for junior. This compares with an advisory fee of possibly $5 million. One impact of this disparity in the size of potential fees is a possible conflict of interest. An investment bank's fees are normally success-related, so regardless of the financing fees the incentive for the investment bank is (almost) invariably to advise a client to complete a transaction, and it is unusual for an investment bank to advise against a deal that a client is willing and capable of completing. The conflict may come in the investment bank's advice about which financing structure to use to complete a transaction.

Syndication and restructuring – Zero-sum games

There are a number of areas in investment banking that can be typified by relatively aggressive behaviour, and it is usefully to consider each separately. We have taken two areas that involve situations where the outcome of a transaction can be a "zero-sum game" or the distribution of a finite pool of value, increasing the incentives for aggressive behaviour.

Syndication

In the sale of securities (whether a primary or secondary issue), a syndicate made up of a number of investment banks may be appointed. They will be sharing a defined percentage fee (the percentage will vary according to *inter alia* the type of security concerned). The total fee is therefore largely fixed, and the vast majority of the fee is shared among the syndicate, based on their success in selling the security and on whatever is agreed among themselves and with the client. Issues such as which investment bank is able to market to which institution therefore become extremely important in maximising the revenue for each individual investment bank. Behaviour among syndicate members can become both aggressive and highly imaginative. This is an area where the temptations to move over the ethical line are relatively great. It is difficult to see how the line management of a syndication department could be expected to manage such a department entirely ethically in the context of generally understood aggressive behaviour, unless there was a strong lead from senior management to do so. It is difficult to look at syndication in isolation from other capital market activities, given it is intrinsically part of capital raising, alongside research, sales and trading.

Financial restructuring

Financial restructuring relates to over-leveraged companies that are often faced with some form of default or insolvency. As insolvency regimes are very much country-specific, the detailed nature of restructuring can vary significantly. Restructuring centres around deciding on and agreeing how different stakeholder groups can share the economic value of an entity that is unable to meet all its liabilities. There may be different, defined creditor groups, as well as shareholders and also trade creditors. As with syndication, as there is normally a specifically limited economic value to be assigned, the incentive in such a negotiation is to be unrelenting in order to be effective. Applying the analysis of game theory in this situation would almost certainly support taking an extreme negotiating stance.

The nature of restructuring is different from most forms of transaction, in that parties have to reach a deal, rather than the normal case of two parties both being able to choose whether to reach agreement or not. This dynamic requires aggressive negotiation in order to be successful. Despite the requirement for aggressive negotiation, there is a risk that this can lead to more generally aggressive and abusive behaviour. While an aggressive negotiating style would not be unethical *per se*, there are clearly limitations to the range of ethically acceptably behaviour, where judgement needs to be applied.

There are specific ethical issues to be faced in a restructuring: first, relating to confidential information passed to "restricted" creditors; second, relating to the impact of some negotiating strategies or positions on "hold-out value" on the long-term economic value of a business; and third, relating to fees.

Confidential information

An investment bank receiving confidential information relating to one security may find it affects the value of another. If the second security is not covered by insider dealing laws – such as (unquoted) bank debt – the investment bank may decide that it is legally able to trade in the security. Although it has a commercial agreement not to do so, the agreement is a legal contract, so the bank is liable for civil damages if it is breached, and from a commercial perspective the bank is then able to choose whether to breach the contract. This approach effectively simply places a cost on complying with a contract, rather than assuming any ethical obligation to comply. Such behaviour is certainly aggressive, and probably not mainstream in investment banking. Morally it is dubious, as it involves breaching an existing commitment (not to trade on the basis of confidential information). This practice may be more prevalent among hedge funds than investment banks.

Hold-out value

There are occasions when the owner of a particular security may be able to benefit beyond the pure economic value of their securities, as a result of other rights or entitlements, such as the right to withhold consent. This is sometimes referred to as "hold-out value". This can be seen, on the one hand, as tantamount to extortion and, on the other, as upholding contractual rights. There is a fundamental difference of opinion between the US view of the "sanctity" of a contract, and the European view of the spirit of an agreement, which also reflects some jurisprudence differences in the different continents. It is apparent that the power to consent or veto has a value, which is in certain circumstances greater than is often understood when it is granted by an issuer of securities. The fact that this value (or power) exists and is used does not render such use necessarily unethical, although at times when its use goes clearly beyond any reasonable exercise of a contractual right it is likely to raise ethical problems. An additional question should be posed to the original advisers on debt structuring, in terms of whether they have fully explained the "option value" being conceded by potentially allowing such a hold-out.

Margin calls

Similarly, borrowing against securities raises specific problems. These relate to the power given to a lender to divest the security under certain circumstances. The lender, under these circumstances, may only be concerned with making whole the original loan. This can result in inefficiently timed (and obviously so) sales of securities, at the worst possible terms for the borrower, who therefore experiences significant economic harm. As with the discussion on hold-out value, the borrower may have given away value without realising how significant it is, not appreciating the significant option value associated with decisions to sell (or buy) securities. In practice, the market can anticipate some major margin calls or defaults, and consequently the price of affected securities is likely to be adversely affected. Under these circumstances, the duty of the lender is to recover the debt rather than speculate on the future value of the security, leading to apparently economically inefficient behaviour, to the detriment of the borrower. Although the behaviour of lenders in such situations is typically not sympathetic to borrowers (and sympathy would not be expected), and is potentially injurious to them, it is difficult to see this as unethical *per se*. However, where the impact of a failure to pay a "margin" can be disproportionately damaging, there is an ethical duty to minimise the economic damage, where it is possible to do so.

Restructuring fees

Fees paid during a restructuring are at the expense of a broad group of stakeholders, including shareholders and creditors. However, the fees of investment banking advisers may be agreed by a single group of shareholders or creditors, rather than by all affected parties. In such circumstances, there is less incentive for clients to fully negotiate fees, as they are, in effect, only paying part of the fee of the advisers they engage. There are many examples of the fees of restructuring advisers being reduced by US bankruptcy courts, which may in part reflect the less competitive nature of the original fee negotiation.

This chapter has highlighted a number of issues of ethical concern regarding investment banks' dealings with clients. In a highly competitive industry there are strong incentives for firms – and individuals within firms – to push at the boundaries of what is morally acceptable. While this is the reality, there is still a need for high ethical standards, to enable the industry as a whole to operate effectively and engender the trust and confidence required to underpin markets.

Engagement letters

Investment banking agreements with clients to carry out a transaction and to be paid fees are covered in "engagement letters". These have become increasingly complex documents, stating the work to be carried out, fee levels and complex terms and conditions.

Most major corporates have in-house legal expertise, which routinely advises on the terms under which an investment bank is retained. However, this does not remove the ethical burden from investment banks to ensure that the implications of their terms of engagement are properly understood.

In addition to issues over fees and "bait and switch" (discussed on p. 113), there are further issues with possible ethical implications arising from engagement letters. These are (i) the nature of the terms and conditions, and (ii) how the terms and conditions are disclosed.

An investment banking client typically hires an investment bank on account of either a need for specific resource, or because of the investment bank's specialist expertise (notably on advisory assignments) or because of its capacity in capital markets (typically in relation to securities issuance).

Sometimes, the detailed terms and conditions can add costs or a percentage for specific services provided to the client, such as printing or copying, which are in addition to the agreed fee. In these cases, it is important that a client's attention should be actively drawn to such terms.

There are specific concerns surrounding issues normally covered in the terms and conditions within an engagement letter, relating to indemnities and "tails".

These are commercially significant issues, and arguably should not only be in the fine print. The structure of most indemnity wording, giving an investment bank the ability to recover costs from a client under certain circumstances – covering everything other than gross negligence or wilful default – sets a contractual test which is difficult to reach.

A tail gives an investment bank the ability to claim a fee from a transaction sometime after a mandate has expired, whether or not the investment bank has contributed to an eventual transaction. The correct purpose of a tail is to protect an adviser from the early termination of an engagement, after doing substantially all the work but before a transaction closes. However, in some circumstances a tail could give rise to a fee even if an investment bank had not contributed to an eventual transaction, sometimes after the end of a mandate. Given that a tail has a justifiable reason for inclusion in an engagement letter, but nonetheless can also give rise to concerns on the part of a client, it raises issues that should be discussed before an engagement letter is agreed.

The structure and content of investment banking engagement letters can appear to undermine the concept that investment banks are trusted advisers.

Ethical implications for investment banks

- There are three broad areas of ethical concern regarding treatment of clients: conflict of interest, duty of care and, more broadly, truth and honesty.
- Market behaviour, which includes confidence that promises to pay will be honoured, is archetypal good ethical behaviour. This type of behaviour is not central to other areas of investment banking.
- Actively misleading clients is ethically similar to lying.
- Bait and switch, a practice much criticised by clients, is unethical.
- At a stage when an investment bank agrees to carry out an assignment for a client it has a duty of care, specifically to give honest advice, act in the client's interest in the transaction and utilise the investment bank's resources.
- A capital market's department may simultaneously have different relationships with the same institution. It is ethically important that the nature of the duty of care to such a client is understood by the investment bankers concerned.
- Conflicts of interest can be created by incentives to act against a client's interest. Conflicts may not be able to be resolved simply by disclosure and transparency, although they may be part of the resolution of the conflict. Representing two parties in the same transaction will always create a conflict, especially where the fees are asymmetric.
- In marketing and pitching, investment banks should remain aware of ethical constraints when making claims as to expertise, capabilities and track record.
- Commercially significant (or potentially significant) terms that are contained in an engagement letter should be clearly explained to a client.

- Equity research, even when independent, can be misleadingly marketed.
- Although investment banking fees are generally set in a competitive environment, nonetheless the ethics of the proposed fees should be considered where there is reason to believe that the fees may not be fully competitive.
- Behaviour in the more aggressive areas of investment banking, such as syndication and restructuring, raises specific ethical challenges that can only be managed at a senior level in the investment bank, as the incentive for the directly involved bankers will be to maximise their revenue.

Chapter summary

- Markets only work because participants believe their contracts will be honoured. Keeping promises is archetypal good ethical behaviour as it engenders trust.
- There are a number of ethical dilemmas facing investment banking, relating to truth, lying and misleading. Lying, and misleading in such as way as to be equivalent to lying, are unethical.
- It is not reasonable to suggest that a pitch document or sales script should be verified in the same way as a prospectus or information memorandum.
- In pitches:
  - Wording used should not be actively misleading or deliberately untrue.
  - A team presented at a pitch should be genuinely expected (at the time – in transactions situations can change rapidly) to execute the transaction, or the pitch should clearly disclose the team that is to execute the transaction.
  - Special care should be taken in describing conflicts of interest (as opposed to explaining why such conflicts do not exist or are not relevant).
  - The duty of care shown to a client should always be taken seriously, and the resources committed to the client should be made available.
- An investment bank has a duty of care to its clients. Given the range of different activities carried out within an investment bank, the nature of relationships with clients and of the duty of care will vary. A duty of care implies acting in a client's interest in executing a transaction,

giving honest advice and utilising the bank's resources in furthering the client's interest.

- Conflicts of interest are ubiquitous problems in investment banking, and in general the more successful the investment bank, the more conflicts will develop. Being party to information that can be used against a client's best interest, and where there is an incentive to do so, raises serious questions of fairness, honesty and trust.
- The incentives created by advising on a sell-side engagement while simultaneously providing or arranging finance for a buyer provide incentives that undermine an investment bank's duty of care.
- A capital market's department will have a duty of care to different clients in different situations. Ethically, a duty of care will extend beyond fee-paying clients to all clients with which the investment bank trades, albeit the nature of the duty of care may vary.
- The marketing of equity research presents ethical issues regarding its sincerity regarding recommendations, and also regarding the representation of how much research has been undertaken.
- Investment banking fees are generally set in a highly competitive framework. However, ethical concerns may arise in situations where the level of fee is such that a client regrets entering a transaction, where the fee is agreed by a client not properly interested in negotiating the fee or in situations where the client does not fully understand the fee.
- The pressure on bankers responsible for a client or engagement is to agree the highest possible fee. However, where there are ethical considerations, an investment bank should consider the ethics of the fees being sought and not simply seek to optimise its own income.
- There are specific ethical issues relating to transactions that are "zero-sum games", such as syndications or restructuring, which incentivise aggressive behaviour and negotiation. These present particular ethical problems.
- The structure and content of engagement letters can undermine the idea that an investment bank seeks to be a "trusted adviser". Investment banks should ensure that all fees and cost-recoveries and commercially significant conditions (notably tails and indemnities) are properly understood before an engagement letter is agreed.

Under what circumstances is it worthwhile for an investment bank to risk a conflict of interest by acting in two roles in the same transaction? Is there an ethical rule that governs this, or is the level of fee more important?

8
Ethical Issues – Internal

Investment banks face a series of ethical issues relating to their own businesses, focused on managing resources and employees. These include abusing company funds, discrimination, accepting or providing undue hospitality and poor management behaviour. In addition, there can be ethical issues surrounding levels of remuneration, notably where an investment bank is funded by a Government.

Internal ethical issues

As well as practices that cause ethical problems involving clients, there are also issues of long-standing practice in some investment banks, or departments, which raise ethical questions:

- Abuse of the company's (and therefore shareholders') resources.
- Discriminatory, notably sexist, culture. This can include the review, promotion and compensation culture within an investment bank or department as well as client entertainment (such as visiting lap-dancing clubs).
- Accepting or offering undue hospitality: the cost of some corporate hospitality packages appears costly, but is tiny compared with the size of fees for a large acquisition or capital raising. Entertainment packages for semi-finals or finals at Wimbledon or the US Open can cost in excess of $5,000 (much more than the face cost of the tickets). The intent of providing corporate hospitality is normally to solicit further business.
- Abusive (bullying) management behaviour.
- Levels of remuneration, especially for an investment bank funded by a Government.
- Tax, and tax optimisation.

Abuse of resources

Out-of-pocket expenses

An area of ethical concern, especially for senior management, is abuse of company resources. This has become more public through scrutiny of the run-up to the financial crisis. Given both the responsibility and time commitment of senior bankers, investment banks have to put in place support structures to enable investment bankers to work effectively, at the same time as trying to maintain a home life. This can include the provision of transport (car services, and even at times private planes) and paying for entertaining clients at prestigious sporting events (such as Wimbledon or the New York Open). Such provision can easily be abused by charging the investment bank or clients for meals or transport that have not been incurred on company business.

This type of action is sometimes the result of a lapse of attention, but is sometimes quite deliberate.

There are specific issues that arise when travelling on business, related to which expenses can legitimately be charged to a client, and which to the employer. All investment banks have different codes of practice relating to travel costs, but these are less clear when involving costs recharged to a client.

A significant area of concern is the way costs are recharged to clients during the course of a transaction. It is normal to agree with an advisory client that out-of-pocket expenses will be recharged, whether or not a transaction is successful. This can include meals and transport required when employees are working late. Given that investment bankers, particularly at a junior level, routinely work very long hours, the costs involved can be significant over the course of a lengthy assignment. Some investment bankers are not fastidious about genuinely recording recharged costs accurately, and will simply look for a client or transaction to which a dinner or a journey home late at night can be charged. The ethics of this are clear: charging unjustified expenses is both a breach of trust by the investment banker, and is effectively theft from the client. In some cases, an investment bank actively encourages as many costs as possible to be recharged to clients – this can significantly improve profitability, and therefore potentially enhance the bonus pool. If a transaction is unsuccessful, the out-of-pocket costs are likely to be a very small percentage of the overall fee, so they can often be overlooked. However, it does not change the ethical issue of stealing from a client by charging unmerited expenses.

Personal account trading/investing

Many investment bankers at all levels will actively trade securities and make personal investments. The main potential abuse here is the misuse of proprietary information through insider dealing. Such investments are governed by tightly controlled compliance rules, generally relating to an investment bank in totality, and not just to an individual. In this area, it is unlikely that there are issues that are unable to be dealt with by normal compliance procedures, which are aimed principally in this instance at preventing conflicts of interest.

The major concern remaining over personal account trading is whether it distracts investment bankers from paying full attention to their jobs – this is more a professional than an ethical concern. It is also now required that equity analysts disclose any personal account holdings relating to investment recommendations.

Hospitality and corporate entertainment

Investment banks often provide – and feel compelled to provide – valuable corporate entertainment. This can vary from a meal at an expensive restaurant to entertainment at tennis or golf championships, or even a skiing, hunting or fishing trip lasting a number of days.

Corporate entertainment is designed to solicit client business. It is accepted by clients, who have their own fiduciary duties. It is also sometimes presented as a "thank you" for business that has been received.

While corporate hospitality in itself may not be ethically problematical, the nature of the hospitality can be, both in terms of its effect on relationships with clients and in terms of its impact on employees.

The giving of corporate gifts is generally now restricted by company policies to relatively low levels, and is increasingly the focus of legislation aimed at preventing bribery. If entertainment is designed to encourage a client to award business in a way it would not otherwise have done, purely on account of the entertainment, that would constitute bribery, and be unethical. However, most entertainment is more sophisticated than that: it gives a longer opportunity than a normal meeting to talk informally to a client, and it is the increased confidence in an adviser, salesman, analyst or trader, which goes with knowing them better, which makes the client more likely to award business. This is entirely legitimate, and should be ethical in most situations.

At some stage in the spectrum of entertainment, from a coffee at Starbucks to a holiday in the Caribbean, there is a point where the entertainment becomes difficult to justify and akin to bribery. Hard and fast rules are difficult to precisely determine, and this is therefore an area where careful ethical judgement needs to be applied.

Recent legal reform in the UK, and the Bribery Act 2010,[1] have changed the basis of legal consideration of bribery. As well as dealing with bribery by individuals, the Act has also introduced a new offence, of a corporation failing to prevent a bribe being paid on its behalf.

One of the difficulties faced in any business that is highly international, like investment banking, is that it raises ethical issues that may be approached in different ways in different cultures. For this reason, a number of businesses whose workforce or client base is international have turned to anthropologists and those with expertise in religion for advice about cultural norms and religious practices. So, too, has the academic study of business ethics broadened to look beyond its Western philosophical underpinning. One area of particular concern from a cross-cultural perspective is the issue of gifts and bribery. What, in some cultures (particularly Western) can be seen as bribery, in others (particularly Eastern) might be regarded as politeness and an acceptable expression of a business relationship.

From an ethical perspective, where such uncertainty arises there are three key considerations that relate to intent and consequences:

- What is the motive of the giver? Is it to gain advantage by compromising someone, or is it an expression of thanks or cultural politeness?
- What impact does it have on the recipient? Does the gift go beyond what he or she might expect to receive in such a situation?
- How is it perceived by others? Will they regard it as crossing the line of acceptability?

In this respect, virtuous behaviour is informed by both deontological principles (motives) and consequentialist ethics (outcomes).

Discriminatory behaviour

Major investment banks actively seek to operate a meritocracy, in order to succeed in very competitive markets by employing the best possible investment bankers. However, given the existing cultures of many investment banking departments, there are occasions where gender discrimination can and has become inculcated, notably on dealing floors.

In "capital markets" departments, entertaining may focus on relatively junior clients, who may have significant power to reward salesmen and analysts through placing orders or voting in surveys. In a few cases, such clients may like to be entertained in a way that is difficult to justify ethically, but which is commercially worthwhile. Female employees in an investment bank in particular may see this practice as not only as distasteful but discriminatory. The typical example of this would be visits to table-dancing clubs. Pornography, and the exploitation of people, is unethical (viz. religious restrictions on investment in companies involved in pornography). However, in some cases, it can be very successful for the investment banker happy to entertain a client in this way. In reality, this practice is unlikely to stop until the costs of dealing with litigation for discrimination become greater than the commercial benefit, at which stage investment banks will actively proscribe this type of entertainment.

There have also been prominent incidents of an investment banking department taking staff to table-dancing clubs, or the equivalent. This practice is more widespread in the US and parts of Asia than it is in London and Europe (excluding Russia and parts of central Europe), and is not restricted to investment banking, but occurs in other professional services sectors and industrial sectors.

The ethics of table dancing are essentially the same as those of other forms of female pornography. Ethical concerns about pornography centre on the objectification of women, that is, focusing on women for their (potential) sexual value, rather than their other attributes, in this case their professional capabilities as investment bankers. Such objectification is not consistent with a workplace, suppliers and clients that include women. At the extreme, it can lead to harm being caused to women, although this does not normally appear to be a (widespread) problem in investment banks.

Pornography is an area of ethical concern for all the major religions, regardless of their specific approach to women.

There are counterarguments relating to freedom of speech, and by association to behaviour, claiming that women are free to make a decision to be the objects of pornography (and sexual desire). The danger with these arguments is that they do not fully take into account the damage done to other women, who may be objectified as a result of pornography. Arguments against restricting pornography on the grounds of free speech are less relevant for an investment bank than for a Government – an investment bank does not have to reflect constitutional implications as it sets its internal policies.

Investment banks typically have stringent policies in place to encourage diversity and equality. It is apparent that these policies either break down or are unworkable on occasion, notably in this context, where dealing floors are concerned and where clients and employees are young and often single. Failing to take equality seriously can lead to missed opportunities to spot the most talented employees, and to relate to sections of the client-universe. It can be commercially damaging as well as unethical. However, it is clear that the very male-dominated culture of trading floors can be highly effective, and difficult to alter.

Management behaviour

There is less formal training of senior management in investment banking than in some other sectors, notably the manufacturing industry, although there may be more than in, for example, politics.

Identification and promotion to a position such as head of research or head of corporate finance tends to be based on one of four things: (i) outstanding professional success (i.e., in the role of an equity analyst or in M&A), (ii) administrative capability, (iii) leadership capability or (iv) ability to manage internal politics.

Managers can find themselves taking decisions on issues relating to employees for which they have little relevant training; however, they will normally have high-quality professional support from departments such as human resources, compliance and legal. The converse of this is that investment banking can be very much a meritocracy, although this varies between institutions and between departments in an investment bank.

The power that senior management holds over their employees is substantially greater than in most industries. This notably relates to decisions over bonuses – which form the vast majority of compensation for all but the most junior bankers. Investment banking in many areas has a "patronage" culture, encouraging junior bankers to be loyal to their managers.

The risk is that senior management abuse this power, which normally happens in one of two ways:

- first, by taking subjective likes and dislikes to individuals not based on professional performance;
- second, by not taking management responsibilities seriously.

The first of these raises clear ethical issues, and is the basis of discriminatory behaviour; the second is more typically an issue of poor management.

The attitude of investment banks towards their employees can, in practice, be highly impersonal and not take account of individuals. Investment banking is a highly competitive world where the talented will rise to be successful, and a high attrition rate is expected. Leaving newly recruited analysts to be managed by newly promoted associates often leads to institutionalised bullying. This can lead to very high rates of resignation from some departments. There is a level of abuse of analysts in advisory departments that can be put down to poor management, but there is also a level which reaches institutionalised bullying.

There are also management issues associated with those wishing to benefit from successful business practices without risking being associated with possible failure. This can mean that managers allow abusive practices to become widespread and widely understood, without ever formally acknowledging them. This can be a management failure as much as an ethical issue.

Remuneration

The remuneration of bankers and investment bankers has become a public, political and media issue, due to the apparent greed shown by investment bankers in light of the depths of the financial crisis.

The level of fees paid in investment banking supports remuneration (typically called "compensation" in investment banking) at levels not normally seen in most other industries. Levels of compensation have generally been defended by investment banks, and heavily criticised by the media, politicians, trade unions and the public at large.

Political action has been taken to restrict (some) bankers' pay in Europe and the US. On 31 July 2009, the US House voted by 237–185 to restrict bankers' bonuses. Although the vote was not passed by the Senate and therefore did not become law, it showed the level of concern over pay, and the extent to which compensation in the investment banking industry is now a political issue. Subsequently, on 23 October 2009 (for the top 25 employees) and 13 December 2009 (for the remainder of the top 100 employees) the US executive-pay czar ("Special Master for Executive Compensation") appointed by the US Treasury Department put measures in place to put limits on the cash compensation for the top 100 employees at $500,000 for four companies bailed out by the US Government, including a major bank, Citi. On 30 June 2010, the EU agreed to place limits on bankers' bonuses for the following year. Bankers would be limited to receiving no more than 30 per cent of bonuses immediately and in cash, with a 20 per cent limit for larger bonuses. The remainder of bonus payments were linked to long-term performance, with 50 per cent to be paid in shares. In addition, these rules would also extend to hedge funds. These rules did not seek to limit the overall size of bonuses paid to bankers.

Project Merlin is an agreement between the UK Government and the major UK banks. The agreement covers lending, tax, pay and "other economic contributions", including a contribution of £1 billion of capital to the UK's Business Growth Fund.[2]

The major UK banks stated that they "understood the public mood" and would follow responsible pay practices in 2010 and beyond, notably through shareholder engagement. The aggregate bonus pools in 2010 would be lower than 2009.

As well as disclosing the remuneration of their executive directors, the banks agreed to disclose the remuneration of their five highest paid "senior executive officers". Each bank committed to engage with its "major institutional shareholders" on pay policy and practice each year. This is in addition to the current practice – a legal requirement in the UK – for shareholders to vote on the company's remuneration report.

One effect of taxes and limits on bonuses has been to increase base salaries for some levels of investment bankers, notably for managing directors, since base salary levels have been modest compared with total remuneration. To some outside observers, this trend has looked cynical, or even like tax avoidance. However, an increase may bring base salaries more in line with other sectors, as investment banking base salary levels have been very low compared with, for example, those for senior executives in industry and partners in law or accountancy firms. Another reported effect of legal attempts to limit bankers' pay, and of increased taxes, has been investment bankers relocating to jurisdictions with a less restrictive approach to bankers' remuneration.

Payments for failure, which have been a specific source of political and popular concern, such as pay-offs for departing executives, are not a typical feature of investment banks, other than for executive board members, where ethical issues are similar to those in other industrial sectors that have "golden parachute" arrangements. However, investment bankers receiving high levels of compensation can bank significant sums personally in respect of successful transactions, and subsequently their employer can suffer significant losses from the after-effects of the same transactions, with no ability to claw back bonuses already paid. Many (probably all) investment banks have paid significant proportions of bonuses in shares, or in "deferred shares", in order to encourage loyalty and a shareholder mentality, thereby giving employees and shareholders common incentives. This has its limitations, however. For an investment banker earning high levels of bonus, there are two factors that undermine this premise: first, a successful investment banker is able to find alternative highly remunerated employment elsewhere; and second, the level of cash compensation is sufficient to allow the investment banker to enjoy an attractive lifestyle even if the share proportion of compensation is written-off. The incentives in investment banking actively encourage risk-taking, often at the expense of ethical behaviour.

Claiming credit – Managing the internal review process

There are also ethical issues in how investment bankers behave within the advisory departments of an investment bank in order to maximise their own remuneration. Investment banks will pay investment bankers based on their contribution to transactions. As part of the annual review process, investment banks will assess the contribution of individual investment bankers to revenue-earning transactions, especially for senior bankers. In general, the more senior the banker, the more their remuneration will reflect their personal contribution. Investment bankers will provide details of their role in completed transactions. They, moreover, also communicate with senior management following an individual transaction in order to explain their role.

This process can give rise to unethical behaviour by some investment bankers. This can include making exaggerated claims in annual reviews and following individual completed transactions or trades regarding their own involvement. To senior management, it can sometimes be relatively difficult to assess who has primarily been responsible for a transaction being originated and executed, and who has been a more or less superfluous member of the team. Following a successful transaction or a successful year, there can be an incentive for some investment bankers to spend more time managing their own review process than in originating and executing business. This can lead to unethical behaviour, notably involving misleading senior management regarding revenue generation. The results of this can be that the investment banker concerned is paid in excess of what is merited, but also that other investment bankers are under-remunerated.

Is remuneration an ethical issue?

Remuneration can be considered an ethical issue from a number of perspectives, notably relating to fairness (i.e., equity and distributive justice), and also relating to the issue discussed on p. 24 of investment banks receiving a "free-ride". There is an argument that the banking crisis was caused by greed. This has been advanced by, among others, former UK Prime Minister Gordon Brown. It can be argued that the cause of the financial crisis (in the UK) was excess bank bonuses resulting in a deficiency in bank capital. This argument contends that the payment of bonuses left the banking sector short of capital, and therefore the financial crisis was (at least in part) the result of greed.

There are ethical arguments supporting controlled levels of pay for highly paid employees. For example, in 2010, in *The Ethics of Executive Remuneration: a Guide for Christian Investors*,[3] the Church Investors' Group (CIG) in the UK called for a limit of remuneration at 75 times the remuneration of the lowest paid 10 per cent of employees in a company. The logic for this particular number was unclear in the CIG guide, and it could give rise to some bizarre effects: for example, a company that consciously and responsibly employs low-paid workers rather than contracting out services such as cleaning, would have limits placed on pay which would not be reflected by a competitor who contracted out all low-paid services purely on the basis of cost.

Investment banks typically have very commercial cultures. With (historically) low base salaries and discretionary bonuses, many investment bankers feel insecure regarding their jobs and their remuneration. In addition to this, many investment banks have a focus both on caring for their employees and on encouraging productivity, which can be in conflict at times. Consequently, investment bankers may not be fully confident that they will continue to be employed and/or well remunerated in the medium term, and as a result see each bonus as both earned or deserved, as well as potentially not repeated.

1 Timothy 6:10 "The love of money is the root of all evil."

The attitude of the major religions to high pay is not consistent: the Christian churches, especially the Protestant churches, are generally more concerned about high levels of remuneration and personal wealth than Judaism and Islam. For example, the words of Jesus in the New Testament frequently warn of the dangers of wealth.

All major religions encourage charitable giving. There are numerous examples of investment bankers who are also philanthropists, and many investment banks also have (normally relatively modest) philanthropic or charitable giving programmes.

Provided that compensation for employees is justifiable based on their own – and their firm's – performance, high levels of remuneration are not normally unethical. Ethical problems do arise, however, in the following circumstances:

- When one group of employees is remunerated unfairly over another.
- When employees are remunerated unfairly in relation to shareholders.

With regard to the first point, which has come into prominence with the growing disparity in many sectors between executive pay and that of lower earners, it is hard to determine what is a just and fair disparity. Of considerable help here is Rawls' theory of justice. A guiding principle, using this theory, is the recognition that all employees in some way contribute to a firm's performance and so pay across the firm should reflect this, as well as rewarding the distinctive contribution of particular groups or individuals. One possible practical implication is that when profits are shared, those who are paid least (including ancillary staff) should receive a reward so that they, too, are better off.

Within an investment bank, compensation can be partly objective, but also tends to be based on a system of patronage. Heads of department or teams have a major input into decisions on compensation. Annual reviews of employees can be tactical, with few senior bankers grading anyone in their oversight as at or below average for their firm. The level of influence that senior bankers can have over the compensation of their employees is very unusual, and creates an atmosphere where junior bankers and those approaching a promotion are unlikely to criticise their managers (although there can, of course, be exceptions to this). This is in contrast to most sectors, where employee remuneration follows well-understood guidelines, annual performance appraisals are relatively procedural and performance-related elements of pay are often a fraction of base salaries.

Remuneration and bonus pools in public ownership

Ethical problems also come into areas of public ownership/investment. With regard to remuneration, the payment of bonuses has come under particular scrutiny as a result of the financial crisis. This is due both to the scales of bonuses – which can be into millions of pounds or dollars – and to the argument that they promote a culture of short-term gain within banking, rather than looking to the longer term. With regard to the latter, there has been pressure on firms to pay a higher proportion of bonuses in shares.

The financial crisis has also raised an unusual ethical dilemma – should state-supported bankers receive bonuses?

It would undoubtedly be ethical for an investment banker to renounce a bonus at a time when their employer was temporarily Government-funded, especially if they were unprofitable. It would not, however, be unethical *per se* to accept such a payment under most circumstances.

As a result of the financial crisis, a number of Governments have taken stakes in major banks and investment banks, mainly in order to ensure that financial systems continue to operate effectively. Where stakes have been taken in commercial banks, these banks have sometimes had major investment banking operations (e.g., RBS, Citi).

There has been significant political and media attention on paying bonuses when in receipt of Government funding. There are conflicting arguments on whether it is appropriate for a bank or investment bank to pay high (or any) bonuses while effectively being rescued from bankruptcy with public money:

- It is reasonable to assume that in reality an investment bank will lose high-calibre bankers, and therefore reduce shareholder value, if it is to restrict pay to levels below market levels. However, it is unclear whether this would be the case if, for example, such restrictions were only put in place for a single year.
- Investment bankers should not be cushioned from "economic reality" at a time when Governments are cutting services to the majority of the population.

As a major – if not controlling – shareholder, in reality a Government could effectively veto planned bonus payments. The repercussions of this could be significant, in terms of significantly increasing the ability of competitors to poach the best investment bankers. However, as with other state-funded enterprises there is inevitably an aggressive negotiation on major issues of expenditure between ministers and executives. In addition, if a Government accepts the first argument above, that an investment bank will lose value for the Government if it fails to pay adequate bonuses, then there may be a difference between the Government's public statements and its behaviour as a shareholder. Governments have conflicting priorities, including, in many countries, seeking re-election. There may be a difference between public statements and actions taken by a Government. Public, and media, concern over the behaviour of investment banks and bankers' remuneration is, possibly for the first time, a significant popular and political issue.

In addition, a Government has conflicting priorities, such as maximising tax revenues and reducing unemployment, both of which may affect how it deals with the investment banking sector. International competition for investment banks to be headquartered in a country appears to be increasing, and this will form part of political considerations. The location of a bank's headquarters can bring with it tax revenue, highly skilled jobs and ongoing economic benefits.

In current cases, where Governments own major stakes in investment banks, it is unlikely that they would wish to retain such stakes indefinitely. Therefore, their aims will be, first, to stabilise the financial system and, second, to maximise the recovery of the capital invested to achieve the required stability.

It used to be the case that investment bankers argued that they deserved such high salaries due to the riskiness of their profession and the lack of job security. It has also been argued that investment bankers "deserve" their high levels of compensation as a result of their financial contribution to their employers – bonus pools were based on a payout ratio, meaning that shareholders (sometimes the same people as the investment bankers) also benefitted from this success.

The argument that investment bankers deserve high levels of compensation irrespective of the financial performance of their employers is one which is not novel. This has been current internally within investment banks. For example, where an investment bank performed poorly overall, it would nonetheless seek to provide some type of "market" level of compensation to a relatively small number of investment bankers, who were seen as either most productive (in terms of revenue generation) in the previous year or as most important to delivering revenue in the next year. Where an investment bank was part of a larger banking group (akin to RBS), this could happen with a transfer of funds between departments.

Where a Government is the controlling shareholder in a bank, then it is very much the Government's decision whether to award bonuses, whether high or not. A Government is in the position, ethically, to reach a reasonable decision on this issue – to view the long-term value of its investment. Government decisions can encompass ethical considerations as well as other concerns. A decision would be expected to be based (presumably) to a large extent on the advice given by the bank's management as well as on political considerations.

A further question relates to whether it is ethical for an investment banker to accept a bonus payment under circumstances where a bank has been "rescued" by public money. Whereas board members under such circumstances sometimes renounce bonuses or donate them to charities, unlike board members most investment bankers have (relatively) modest base salaries and rely on bonus payments each year. It is also generally less painful for a successful, senior banker to forsake a year's bonus than for a relatively junior banker.

Political considerations are clearly subject to popular concerns. Ethics are also looked at in the context of society as a whole, and ethical considerations will inevitably reflect the wider society's concern over what is ethical and unethical, including, at the present time, remuneration. The weight given to these wider concerns will depend to some extent on how ethics are approached, but both duty-based and utilitarian ethics would clearly indicate that remuneration can be a genuine ethical concern.

Tax

Investment banks actively manage their tax affairs, as do companies in other sectors. As part of this, investment banks may seek to reduce corporation or payroll taxes, where there are legal mechanisms and incentives to do so. Given the extreme complexity of tax in many jurisdictions, it is not always possible or ethically required for an individual tax payer – whether a corporation or an individual – to decide on the intent of individual pieces of tax legislation. Tax optimisation is not unethical in itself. However, payment of taxes is necessary to support Governments and tax optimisation can, under some circumstances, become abusive and unethical.

Taxation of corporates and individuals raises some specific ethical questions. Most major corporations actively manage their tax affairs to reduce the "effective rate" of taxation. Many investment banks look for tax-efficient ways of remunerating employees. Some investment banks offer tax-related services to corporate clients or buy tax losses or gains – Barclays Capital is especially well-known in this context.

There are obvious arguments that paying tax supports parts of society that we have a duty to support, such as health care, education and policing. Also, tax supports Government activities that provide benefits to underprivileged parts of society. Charitable giving is a basic tenet of Christianity, Judaism and Islam, and Government spending includes activities that might be considered to be charitable. However, in some countries tax also supports activities to which we might object (such as wars, oppression of minorities and so on), and is ultimately too complex to relate to an obligation to support charitable activities. In addition, a Government may be a less efficient spender of charitable giving than many Non-Governmental Organisations (NGOs), who typically spend around 80 per cent of the money they receive on the causes they support (a significant proportion of the remaining 20 per cent relates to fundraising, which does not have an equivalent cost for Government). This is because a Government may have to balance complex political considerations rather than focus purely on the delivery of direct benefits from its spending.

Tax is subject to detailed codes and it is not normally practical for individuals and corporate bodies to determine which elements of the appropriate tax code should or should not apply to them. This is especially the case for corporates or investment funds whose directors have fiduciary duties that may entail consideration of legitimate tax optimisation.

Investment banks and other financial institutions have internal tax structuring departments, which are responsible for corporate tax planning and actively engineer group holding and investment structures that are designed to minimise tax charges. An institution will periodically seek the participation of a third party institution to facilitate these arrangements. This occurs as a normal part of corporate tax planning. To further optimise these opportunities, specialist teams may be employed to actively seek opportunities for arranging funding and investment structures in such a way as to maximise the benefit for the institution.

Institutions typically have a target ETR (effective tax rate) which the group tax department is required to maintain on a global basis. The tax department has a number of mechanisms available to maintain this target including the "trading" of tax capacity in the market. The buying and selling of tax capacity is normally conducted via specialist teams outside the tax department itself.

Most, if not all, major banks and companies either have specific teams in place to negotiate and execute structured finance transactions or are known to participate in structured finance transactions. This is widely prevalent business practice, and at least arguably required by directors' fiduciary duties.

As to at which point tax avoidance becomes tax evasion, that is ultimately for the tax authorities (such as HMRC in the UK, the IRS in the US) to decide. There are now very well-prescribed disclosure requirements in the UK and the US, which apply not only to the participants in any structured trade but also to the promoters and brokers: new tax optimisation schemes are disclosed in some jurisdictions in advance and, in effect, are being pre-cleared. Tax authorities frequently amend tax codes to close the door on any particular arrangement that they consider egregious, and they are ordinarily engaged in ongoing negotiations as regards reaching a settlement on the outcome of the tax planning activities of any given institution.

It is fair to say that there are degrees of appropriateness as regards the nature of transactions aimed at tax optimisation. Some are more aggressive than others.

Investment banks may also seek to use tax structures to reduce payroll taxes, particularly in the payment of bonuses. Many loopholes that have been used in the past – for example, paying bonuses in the form of gold bullion or fine wine – have now been closed by tax authorities. Investment banks will continue to explore ways to manage payroll taxes – one of their major costs – for the benefit of their shareholders and employees, while this is permitted by tax authorities. Attempts to reduce such costs that are not legitimate can result in significant fines being imposed by the tax authorities.

As a comparison, many individual taxpayers use some forms of tax "avoidance". For example, individuals who contribute to employer-sponsored retirement plans with pre-tax funds are engaging in tax avoidance because the amount of taxes paid on the funds when they are withdrawn is usually less than the amount that the individual would owe today. Furthermore, retirement plans allow taxpayers to defer paying taxes until a much later date, which allows their savings to grow at a faster rate. Charitable donors may receive a tax break (in the US), or in the UK those who use Gift Aid may also be considered to be adopting some form of "avoidance"; for example, if they give money to areas that would not be funded by the Government, such as development aid in Africa or local charities supporting children, minority groups or the elderly.

In their statement on Project Merlin, the four major UK banks agreed to follow "both the spirit and the letter of the tax law" and comply with HMRC's (the UK tax authority) UK Code of Practice.

Fiduciary duties require directors of a company to make decisions in the interests of the company. This means (explicitly in some jurisdictions such as the UK, implicitly in other jurisdictions) that directors have to make decisions based on their impact on the long-term value of the company. A reduction or increase in tax payments can have a major influence on value, as it reduces profits and cash available either for reinvestment or to be paid as dividends. It is therefore an implication of fiduciary duties that directors should seek to optimise a company's tax affairs.

Ethical implications for investment banks

- There are internal issues that present a challenge to investment banks, and are culturally important to resolve if an overall change in behaviour is sought.
- Issues relate both to abusing client trust (e.g., recharging unjustified expenses), and abusing company or shareholder resources.
- Remuneration for investment bankers directly supported by Government funding raises specific issues: the level of an investment banker's compensation becomes more difficult to justify under these circumstances, and the ethics of negotiating bonuses more questionable.
- Investment banks, like other companies, seek to optimise their tax payments. This is not in itself unethical, provided it is not executed in an abusive way. Directors' fiduciary duties arguably require tax optimisation in order to increase a company's "long-term value".

Chapter summary

- Investment banks face ethical issues relating to managing resources and employees. These include abusing company funds, discrimination, undue hospitality, management behaviour and remuneration
- Charging unmerited expenses is unethical and is equivalent to stealing from a client.
- Given that insider dealing is illegal, the major practical concern over personal account trading is whether it distracts investment bankers from paying full attention to their jobs.
- At some stage in the spectrum of entertainment, from a coffee at Starbucks to a holiday in the Caribbean, there is a point where the entertainment becomes difficult to justify and akin to bribery.
- International cultural differences have ethical implications.
- Major investment banks actively seek to operate a meritocracy in order to succeed in very competitive markets. However, given the existing cultures of many investment banking departments, there are occasions where gender discrimination can and has become inculcated. The male-dominated culture of trading floors may be very entrenched and difficult to change.
- There is less formal training of senior management in investment banking than in some other sectors.
- Investment banking in many areas has a "patronage" culture. It is unethical for management to act on subjective likes and dislikes of individuals not based on professional performance.

- There are management issues associated with wishing to benefit from successful business practices without risking being associated with possible failure. These can allow abusive practices to become widespread.
- The remuneration of bankers and investment bankers is a public, political and media issue.
- Remuneration can be considered an ethical issue from a number of perspectives, notably fairness and distributive justice, and as relating to investment banks receiving a "free-ride".
- Where a Government is the controlling shareholder in a bank, it is very much the Government's decision whether to award bonuses.
- Tax optimisation is not unethical in itself. However, payment of taxes is necessary to support Governments and tax optimisation can, under some circumstances, become abusive and unethical.
- Fiduciary duties, which require directors to make decisions based on the long-term value of the company, implicitly require companies to optimise tax.

How should a junior or mid-level investment banker flag up a concern about their MD (managing director) behaving unethically, for example towards a client? Can this be done without affecting their employment, promotion or compensation prospects?

9
A Proposed Ethical Framework for Investment Banking

A temptation in business generally is to take a broadly utilitarian approach to ethics: to make a judgement about likely outcomes to assess whether a decision is right or wrong. The financial crisis exposed the risk of such a strategy. Assessing the likely consequences of making a decision can be problematic in many situations, and in the case of financial markets it can be especially difficult. The financial crisis was a call for an appraisal of the moral underpinning of the financial system, and the purpose of this book has been to analyse the day-to-day operations of investment banking from a moral perspective, with the objective of providing clear guidance about how ethics can and should be applied to this important economic activity.

We have argued for a pragmatic, pluralist approach to ethics in investment banking, in which deontological and consequentialist principles go alongside cultivating virtuous behaviour in the workplace, but where deontological ethics take precedence in order to give clear guidelines about what is good, acceptable or unacceptable behaviour from an ethical point of view.

In our survey of investment banking, we have highlighted some key areas of concern:

- Misinformation
- Mis-selling
- Market manipulation
- Conflicts of interest
- Insider dealing
- Discrimination

We have also identified a number of day-to-day activities where these are likely to come to the fore:

- Credit ratings
- Lending practices
- Investment recommendations
- Short-selling
- Fee-setting
- Pitching for business
- Entertainment and corporate hospitality
- Remuneration
- Tax optimisation

This list is not exhaustive, but is sufficiently long to indicate that ethical issues can – and do – emerge in a wide range of contexts, many of which are common across organisations in all business sectors and some of which are specific to investment banking.

We have also argued throughout this book that, when in conflict, a firm's duties towards its key stakeholders outweigh its own rights. Underlying this ethical principle is a deeper philosophical understanding of the nature and purpose of a business. We believe that the business of a business is to do business – but, to do so sustainably, it must be for the benefit of society at large. In other words, an investment bank exists primarily to provide financial services, and its duties towards others in relation to this take precedence over the rights of its employees and shareholders.

While this view may be controversial in some quarters, we believe this balance between rights and duties is crucial. When firms put their own interests above those of the clients they serve and the markets they trade in, then the values that make markets work can be eroded and serious problems can occur. It can be argued that this was an important element of the financial crisis.

A framework for ethical investment banking

Could an increased focus on ethics actually change behaviour in investment banks, or is it just another form of prescriptive regulation to be avoided when it starts to impact revenue and profits?

We believe that a greater awareness of ethics has the potential to change corporate culture to some extent generally, but if directed and formulated correctly it can have a considerable impact on specific abusive practices and on individual investment bankers whose ethical standards are poor. Successful investment bankers must be focused and determined. They do not routinely break existing securities (or other) laws, or flout corporate policy (when it is clear). If there is a requirement, both internally and externally, for higher ethical standards, then the same successful investment bankers should be able to respond accordingly.

Admittedly, investment banking can be an amoral business, focused on delivering results rather than behaving according to a system of values. At present, different investment banks have subtly (or sometimes markedly) different cultures, suggesting that there are various ways to practise the business of investment banking: some are more "aggressive" in their trading strategies than others, by which we mean they are less likely to place an emphasis on ethical behaviour. Likewise, successful and senior investment bankers approach their jobs in different ways. Within this spectrum, those whose ethical standards are high should be rewarded accordingly, while those who behave unethically should be penalised in some way, to make clear within their organisations that ethics are important and taken seriously. It needs to be clear that the way to be rewarded and promoted includes, at the very least, not breaching ethical codes, and that ethical principles are not yet another set of rules to be side-stepped, subverted or carefully avoided. This requires judgement at all levels of management, and, above all, real determination at the top of investment banks.

Relying on self-regulation by individual firms is not enough. Doing so runs the risk, in a highly competitive environment, of firms fearing that by taking a lead in ethics they will lose their competitive edge and become less profitable – this can be seen by the wiggle room left in Codes of Ethics for an investment bank to be able to relax its ethical standards so as not to behave outside sector norms. Consequently, there needs to be an industry-wide determination to take ethics seriously, as well as outside intervention to create the environment where ethics can make a difference to the investment banking industry.

As we have argued, ethics goes beyond compliance frameworks. Indeed, as many of the issues raised in this book indicate, the existing regulatory system falls short of inculcating the sort of ethical approach to investment banking that we believe is urgently needed. This reflects the speed of innovation in the markets. It is in part because of the legalistic nature of compliance frameworks – encouraging behaviour that complies with the letter of the law. It is also, in part, the complexity and inappropriateness in relation to practical situations that makes the compliance required in most investment banks less than compelling.

In the wake of the financial crisis, and in response to litigation against investment banks and investment bankers, what we believe is required is a straightforward ethical framework for the industry. This should not be seen as a revision of Compliance. Instead, it is an additional way of approaching investment banking, aimed at protecting reputational and long-term value for shareholders and other stakeholders.

Code of Ethics

At the heart of this response is the Code of Ethics. We have been critical of the existing ethical codes of many investment banks, which appear to be of little practical use and come across as self-serving, as they appear to be more about protecting the investment bank's shareholders than protecting clients. Ethics needs to be considered at all levels in the organisation, not just by an internal "ethics committee" or the Legal/Compliance department. Nevertheless, we regard a Code of Ethics that is grounded in good ethical thought and practically workable, as essential. It is hoped that this book will provide a guide for preparing such a document.

In order to be effective, the framework for Codes of Ethics for investment banking should:

- Cover all major areas of investment banking activity.
- Include enough detailed guidance to be of practical use, both to investment bankers and to senior management/boards of directors.
- Not be limited to compliance with current legislation/regulation – regulation lags behind investment banking practice, given the speed with which markets develop, and to be helpful an ethical framework must provide assistance in assessing new and changing practices.
- Provide a framework for determining answers to ethical questions that is flexible enough to work as market conditions, products and practices change.
- Be underpinned by clear, consistent and rigorous thinking on ethics.
- Avoid conflicting, where possible, with religious ethics, or those of other cultures.

It is necessary for a Code of Ethics to be kept as a live and relevant document for all employees of an investment bank. This can be done by requiring each member of staff to certify on a regular basis that they have read the Code and to explain whether they have complied with it. Ideally, this should be done to coincide with financial reporting periods, so that investment banks can report to shareholders on compliance with the

Code. Ultimately, ethical thinking, including a Code of Ethics, needs to be inculcated into the culture of the investment bank.

We set out below a series of specific issues that could be incorporated into revised Codes.

As a guide to thinking ethically, the questions set out in Chapter 3 should be included when asking ethical questions:

1. What values are relevant in the situation, and what bearing will they have in making a decision?
2. What rights are relevant in the situation, and what bearing will they have in making a decision?
3. Who are the stakeholders, and what duties are they owed?
4. What are the likely intended or unintended consequences of taking a decision?
5. What virtues will be developed or compromised by acting in a particular way?

Investment banks require employees to behave ethically. This requires an understanding of what this means in practice. Employees must be prepared to consider and discuss ethical issues.

A Code of Ethics should be transparent. A firm should be willing to state publicly the ethical principles with which it wishes to be identified, and as such should be willing to be held accountable to them.

A Code should provide employees with information about how to identify and address ethical issues, a summary of the investment bank's ethical rights and duties (including shareholders and clients), a clear indication of expectations of behaviour (both externally and internally focused) and a list of commonly occurring ethical problems with information on how these should be handled.

To be relevant, a Code will need to be amended over time to address changes in business practices. However, it should include sufficient detail to be self-standing, rather than only relevant when read with internal documents (although a Code is not going to be useful if it is so detailed that it covers every relevant issue).

An investment bank has ethical rights and duties. These must be understood at all levels within an investment bank. Ethics is not the sole preserve of the board, the compliance department or the legal department, but is the responsibility of every employee.

It is unethical for management of an investment bank at any level to encourage any action that breaches the Code of Ethics, either through active encouragement or through turning a blind eye. Where there are situations where a breach of the Code of Ethics is likely, for example where there is a conflict between different provisions of the Code, the potential breach needs to be identified and resolved using the principles set out in the Code.

The Code must clearly set out the investment bank's ethical rights and duties.

An investment bank has ethical rights, including the ethical right to use its intellectual property for the benefit of its shareholders. Ethical behaviour does not preclude innovation or the adoption of aggressive strategies that are not unethical.

An investment bank's ethical duties include:

- A duty of care both to clients (who pay fees) and customers (who buy products).
- Duties to its shareholders.
- Duties to employees.
- A duty to behave honestly – to be truthful and not to mislead.
- A duty to act in such a way as to support the markets in which it trades and the Governments in the jurisdictions in which it operates.

An ethical right (including that of using intellectual property) cannot override ethical duties.

All investment banking employees should receive training in ethical thinking, which should include:

- An introduction to ethics.
- The duties of an investment bank, including to its clients and stakeholders.
- An investment bank's rights, including rights to profit from its assets, such as its intellectual property, reputation and market position.
- Frameworks for identifying when a situation has specific ethical connotations and for considering its ethical dimensions.

Employees must respect their duty of care to the investment bank's shareholders. This includes not misusing company property, including proprietary information, for their own gain.

The Code of Ethics must set out how the investment bank approaches its clients, and clearly explain the ethical duties with regard to different groups of clients/customers (if any differentiation is made).

An investment bank should have a policy to determine whether it can act for a specific sector, company or client where there is a reasonable question over whether to do so would be ethical.

The Code of Ethics should explain what standards of behaviour are expected in trading in (regulated) capital markets and trading off-market, and explain how these standards are linked.

Remuneration is an ethical issue. The Code of Ethics should set out the investment bank's approach to remuneration. It would be useful to include reporting measures that can be used to assess how remuneration is handled by the investment bank, such as annually reporting on the payout ratio.

The Code must set out how the bank looks at risk from an ethical perspective. Risk affects a range of stakeholders, including employees, shareholders, clients and counterparties. It is important to set out a framework to consider the ethical implications of decisions regarding use of the investment bank's capital.

The investment bank must have a forum for employees to raise and discuss ethical concerns to ensure they can be resolved satisfactorily without adversely affecting the employee's career, promotion or remuneration.

As part of the Code, established ethical principles could be tailored and applied to investment banking. These should be used to assist day-to-day decision-making. These include the Golden Rule: do to others as you would have them do to you.

Tailoring these concepts would give rise to a number of suggested principles. For example:

> For client-facing investment bankers of an investment banks: if you would not disclose it to your client – or your client would object – you should not be doing it.
> For proprietary trading: if you would not disclose it to your firm's clients, or they or your colleagues would object, you should not be doing it.

One major issue for both an investment bank and for the individual investment banker is to decide how to handle being asked to work on a transaction that an investment banker considers unethical or for a client that they consider unethical. For the investment banker, a flat refusal to work could be prejudicial to their job or bonus prospects, depending on the climate at their company. For the investment bank, it could be problematic to be required to take personal considerations into account when staffing a transaction or a client account. As alternatives, allowing an investment banker to register a formal protest at the time, explaining the basis of the concern and later discussing this in their annual performance review, may encourage and enable consideration of the issue without dramatically prejudicing the individual's career or remuneration. A Code of Ethics should give clear guidance as to how such matters can be raised.

Every employee should study the investment bank's Code of Ethics at least twice a year, or as frequently as the investment bank's financial reporting periods (if the company is publicly traded), confirm that they have read and understood it and indicate areas where they have had difficulty complying, or have been unable to comply, with it. This latter is important – a Code of Ethics cannot be all-encompassing, and it is important that difficulties in keeping to the Code are acknowledged, rather than hidden.

An ethical framework is in addition to applicable legislation and regulation and the investment's bank compliance procedures. Where there is an apparent conflict between ethics and compliance, this should be resolved with care taken to ensure that the full ethical issues, as well as legal and compliance issues, are understood.

A different approach to a Code of Ethics could make an impact in an investment bank genuinely determined to foster an ethical culture. To be useful, a Code needs to go beyond exhortations to be ethical and have integrity, and should explain what this means. It needs to tell investment bankers how to identify and address ethical questions.

External influences – Investment banking ethics committee

We have argued that ethical values in investment banking are unlikely to change without some external impetus. This could come from a legal or regulatory source, but it is unclear whether such an approach would suffer from some of the failings of existing regulation and compliance, notably being based on "prescription" following a precise set of rules. In addition, outside influences risk undermining the benefits of the existing strong cultural values in investment banking, which are often not fully appreciated from the outside.

In order for ethics to be taken seriously in an investment bank, we have argued that it requires an act of determination by senior management, and that it also requires that ethics become part of the culture of the investment bank. Part of the process of inculcating ethical thinking would involve responsibility being taken by leaders of key businesses within an investment bank. This could be done, for example, via an ethics committee, which would look at ethical issues and also be responsible for ensuring appropriate training in ethics for all employees. Some investment banks, such as Goldman, already have an ethics committee, which is able to set ethical policy and has responsibility for reviewing ethics within the investment bank. Large, publicly quoted universal banks typically have a board committee, which includes ethics as one of its areas of scrutiny. For example, HSBC has a Corporate Sustainability Committee whose remit includes environmental, social and ethical issues.

As we have shown in our analysis of Codes of Ethics, investment banks have been wary of committing to ethical standards that are out of kilter with the market, as this could place them in a position to forego business. This makes it difficult to see how an individual investment bank would be able to set ethical standards higher than market norms. The alternative, of reliance on regulation by existing regulators or through new legislation, risks the level of compliance increasing and a failure in understanding how ethics can be inculcated in investment banking.

The solution could lie in self-regulation. Self-regulation (or self-policing) is not always successful, and has limitations. It is also difficult to accept that self-regulation from within an investment bank is likely to be successful on its own: the risk is too high that unilaterally adopting ethical practices against the run of industry norms would prove too costly, in terms of lost profit and thence attrition of staff and clients.

However, a form of self-regulation might offer a solution for the investment banking industry, providing the opportunity to improve ethical standards without compromising the spirit and values of the sector, and without the risk of individual investment banks having to forego profits in order to take an ethical stance. This could be achieved by creating an investment banking ethics committee, which would represent the investment banking sector as a whole and be enabled to review and determine potential ethical breaches. The strongest argument in favour of such an approach working would be the reputational damage done to investment banks that were found to have breached accepted ethical standards.

This model would not be entirely novel. For example, it resembles that already taken in the UK by the investment banking industry in the Takeover Panel, which has its own staff as well as secondees from investment banks and other professions, and is seen externally and internally as an authoritative body. An equivalent investment banking commission on ethics, which would be able to look at ethical concerns and levy meaningful penalties, would be effective – especially so in a sector where reputation has a clear value. This model of self-regulation would have the benefit of remaining close to the underlying spirit and values of investment banking. There are other examples of self-regulation that indicate that this approach could be successful, including that of the legal profession in a number of countries, for example in both the UK and US.

Unusually, given the global nature of capital markets and the leading investment banks, such a body could be created on an international basis. The logistical issues created by an international ethics committee would be significant, but might not be substantially greater than those faced operationally on a daily basis by investment banks.

10
Ethical Issues – Quick Reference Guide for Investment Bankers

In the tables below we have set out the different issues facing invest-ment bankers and their ethical implications, so that they can be quickly and easily identified.

The tables below set out the ethical implications of contentious areas in investment banking, including the main areas highlighted in the financial crisis. They are split between the ethical challenges faced by profession-als in capital markets departments (Table 10.1) and advisory departments (Table 10.2).

These tables cannot aim to be exhaustive and cover every possible ethical dilemma. The ethical advice in them is based on the framework set out principally in Chapter 3 and applied throughout this book.

We have not aimed to comment on practices that are illegal or prevented by regulation already, unless these practices are specifically analysed in the book and are considered ethical or ambiguous (such as short-selling or insider dealing). Lack of reference to a practice therefore should not be taken to indicate that it has particular ethical connotations, either positive or negative.

There are inevitably a number of areas where judgement is required. There can be a fine line between what is ethical and unethical, therefore practices may be ethically ambivalent *per se*, and ethical judgement needs to be exercised.

Table 10.1 Summary of ethical concerns – Capital markets

Activity	Ethical Implications
Conflicts of interest	Depends on details of the situation. Both situations and ethical issues can be complex. Transparency is beneficial, but does not completely resolve ethical issues. Ethical rights of an investment bank do not override ethical duties to a client. Real ethical dilemmas exist when acting for more than one party in a transaction and give incentives for unethical behaviour, potentially breaching the duty of care to a client.
Proprietary trading	Ethical, unless carried out using specifically unethical practices (e.g. market abuse) or creating excessive risk.
Short-selling	Although short-selling has been the subject of significant concern, it is not normally unethical absent any other specific abuse (e.g. insider dealing, market abuse).
Market abuse	Market abuse, such as manipulating stocks, for example by disseminating false rumours, is unethical. However, being able to influence stock prices may be the result of a strong market position, which is not in itself unethical.
Insider dealing	Ambiguous ethically, but in practice normally unethical, specifically as regards abuse of privileged information (although insider dealing is not always unethical *per se*).
Unauthorised trading	Unauthorised trading is unethical. Management giving only informal approval to trade is also unethical.
Mis-selling securities/issuing overvalued securities	Unethical – relies on deliberately misleading, tantamount to lying.
Trading in off-market products	Ethical – in the same way that buying other non-traded financial instruments, such as insurance policies, is ethical. However, similar standards of care and ethics should be adopted as for on-market trading.
Speculation	Short-term trading is not in itself unethical, nor is trading in only minority positions. Where there is an attempt to cause unwarranted economic harm, then it is highly unethical. An alternative definition of speculation, akin to gambling, which

156

156

Table 10.1   (Continued)

Activity	Ethical Implications
	is not normally a market practice, might be considered unethical on the basis that it gives rise to unearned returns, and may create social problems with a wide impact.
Over-leverage	Investment banks are incentivised to raise as much finance as possible. This can be unethical if it results in a client taking on more debt that can realistically be serviced.
Manipulating credit ratings	Ambiguous: if advising an issuer on credit ratings, there is a duty to act in the best interests of the client. However, to actively mislead would be unethical.
Advance warning clients of research	Ambiguous – not necessarily unethical but may breach specific rules/laws, in which case could be unethical by undermining confidence in markets.
Recommendations counter to analyst's personal account investments	Partly a question of analyst credibility; can be unethical.
Exaggerated claims of extent of research undertaken	Unethical as would be misleading.
Misleading claims in pitching	The line between effective marketing and misleading can be very fine. Actively misleading, as opposed to putting a marketing gloss on facts, is unethical.
Engagement letter terms and conditions	Ethical problems exist if major commercial terms are not fully disclosed or are obfuscated, such as a "tail".
Corporate entertainment	Ethical in itself. Unethical if the intent is similar to bribery, that is by encouraging a client to make a decision specifically influenced by the entertainment, or by the scope of the entertainment being excessive (judgement required).
Sexist entertainment (table-dancing clubs etc.)	Unethical – equivalent to pornography in depicting women as sexual objects.
Personal abuse	Normally unethical, may depend on context, that is in some environments personal abuse is relatively commonplace.

| Abusive management practices (bullying) | Unethical – management has a duty of care to employees. Investment banking has a tough, no-compromise ethos, requiring very high levels of dedication from employees, but individuals nonetheless should be respected. This would not just extend to management actions that were injurious to an employee's health and risked causing physical harm. It would also relate to management motivating employees to go beyond reasonable expectations. |

Table 10.2 Summary of ethical concerns arising from the financial crisis – Advisory

Activity	Ethical Implications
Conflicts of interest	Depends on details of the situation. Both situations and ethical issues can be complex. Transparency is beneficial, but does not completely resolve ethical issues. Ethical rights of an investment bank do not override ethical duties to a client. Real ethical dilemmas exist when acting for more than one party in a transaction and give incentives for unethical behaviour, potentially breaching the duty of care to a client.
Misleading claims during a sales process	Unethical if deliberately creating a false impression.
Over-leverage	Investment banks are incentivised to raise as much finance as possible. This can be unethical if it results in a client taking on more debt that can realistically be serviced.
Manipulating credit ratings	Forward projections are inevitably, to some extent, subjective. Normally, an investment bank will understand how a rating agency puts together its ratings. Assisting with attaining a credit rating is entirely ethical, as long as it does not involve presenting false information, or encouraging a client to do so, in which case it is unethical.
Advising ethically contentious sectors	Potentially unethical, but it can be argued that an investment bank should be able to advise any company that carries out legitimate activities. Should be considered as part of an investment bank's Code of Ethics.
Tax optimisation/structuring	Fiduciary duties implicitly require companies to optimise tax affairs. Governments have effectively made tax a complex area, and it is difficult to see why corporations (and individuals) should not be free to actively manage their tax affairs. However, this is an area in which there is scope for unethical behaviour, so it can become unethical if abused.
Bait and switch	Unethical. A client is hiring an advisory team as well as an investment bank. Ethically, it would be expected that the available team should be accurately described.

Misleading claims in pitching	The line between effective marketing and misleading can be very fine. Actively misleading, as opposed to putting a marketing gloss on facts, is unethical.
Engagement letter terms and conditions	Ethical problems exist if major commercial terms are not fully disclosed or are obfuscated, such as a "tail".
Corporate entertainment	Ethical in itself. Unethical if the intent is similar to bribery, that is by encouraging a client to make a decision specifically influenced by the entertainment, or by the scope of the entertainment being excessive (judgement required).
Sexist entertainment (table-dancing clubs etc.)	Unethical – equivalent to pornography in depicting women as sexual objects.
Personal abuse	Normally unethical, may depend on context, that is in some environments personal abuse is relatively commonplace.
Abusive management practices (bullying)	Unethical – management has a duty of care to employees. Investment banking has a tough, no-compromise ethos, requiring very high levels of dedication from employees, but individuals nonetheless should be respected. This would not just extend to management actions that were injurious to an employee's health and risked causing physical harm. It would also relate to management motivating employees to go beyond reasonable expectations.

Postscript

Investment banks and investment banking culture have come under considerable scrutiny and criticism during the financial crisis. As we have sought to show, some of this criticism is justified, some is not.

At its best, investment banking exemplifies value creation, innovation, meritocracy and professionalism. Investment banks publicly espouse good client service, dedication, innovation and continual striving for perfection – all of which can be of significant benefit to clients and employees, and consequently to society at large.

Some of the characteristics displayed by investment bankers – such as intense competitiveness, a measure of arrogance and a desire to make money – are part of the investment banking culture. As we have also sought to show, these can be constructive and beneficial when harnessed effectively to support a client – but they can also sow the seeds for unethical behaviour.

Given the scope and influence of investment banks, where these personal traits are encouraged institutionally and are unconstrained, and things go wrong, tremendous damage can result – as was exemplified by the financial crisis. Of course, not all of the problems associated with the crisis are new or unique to investment banks. The collapse of Barings, the dotcom crash and many other instances demonstrate the complex interaction of ethics and business performance in the financial sector – and similar events will almost certainly occur again. Nevertheless, with greater political scrutiny of investment banking and high levels of public concern, understanding the culture of investment banking and shaping it for the good while addressing its shortcomings have become imperative given the key role investment banks play in economic life.

The approach to managing behavioural standards in investment banks – largely through compliance – has been found wanting in many respects. What we believe is required is a systematic approach to ethics that is applicable to all levels within an investment bank. Our view is that it should combine a regulatory framework with a system of self-monitoring that utilises the modern insights of business ethics. Applying these to produce effective codes of ethics and training programmes is essential – as is leading by example. If management introduces an enhanced approach to ethics, it is important that it plays its full part in this, including clearly requiring ethical behaviour to be maintained even if this results in performance targets being missed.

A greater focus on ethics has the potential to have a significant impact on the integrity of investment banking. We believe that given the competitive nature of the industry, external pressure of some description is likely to be required if investment banking is going to be successful in raising its ethical standards. Ideally, we think this pressure should come from the investment banking sector itself. This will ensure it is most likely to be effective, both because it is more likely to be tailored to meet the needs of the industry and also because it will be associated with a sense of being owned and not imposed.

The aim of this book has been to address the issue of ethics and integrity in investment banking through the use of applied ethics, without harming the unique and beneficial attributes of the investment banking culture. We hope, too, that it will encourage those associated with investment banking to take action and put into place effective codes of ethics and ethical training. Our overall objective is to help equip investment banks to address some of the issues raised by the financial crisis. We hope that, in some way, this book serves this purpose.

Notes

Chapter 1

1. Financial Crisis Inquiry Commission (2011) *Financial Crisis Inquiry Commission Releases Report on the Causes of the Financial Crisis*. As well as publishing the results of its inquiry, the FCIC also published two dissenting opinions by members of the Commission.
2. Independent Banking Commission (2010) *Issues Paper Call for Evidence*.
3. Roger Bootle (2009) *The Trouble with Markets* (London and Boston: Nicholas Brealey Publishing).
4. Gordon Brown (2010) *Beyond the Crash: Overcoming the First Crisis of Globalisation* (London: Simon & Schuster).
5. Benedict XVI (2009) Encyclical Letter *Caritas in Veritate*, Vatican.
6. SEC (2010) *SEC Charges Goldman Sachs with Fraud in Structuring and Marketing of CDO Tied to Subprime Mortgages*.
7. *New York Times*, 20 November 2005 http://www.nytimes.com/2005/11/20/business/yourmoney/20jail.html?pagewanted=all, accessed 8 March 2011.
8. Geraint Anderson http://www.moneyweb.com/mw/view/mw/en/page308878?oid=309416&sn=2009+Detail&pid=287226, accessed 8 March 2011.

Chapter 2

1. Adam Smith (1776) *The Wealth of Nations* (London: W. Strahan and T. Cadell).
2. Adam Smith (1759) *The Theory of Moral Sentiments*.
3. http://www.sec.gov/news/press/2010/2010-59.htm, accessed 8 March 2011.
4. Goldman Sachs (2011) *Business Standards Report*, section v, para A.
5. http://online.wsj.com/article/SB122576100620095567.html, accessed 8 March 2011.
6. Independent Banking Commission (2010) *Issues Paper Call for Evidence*.
7. DTI (2007) *Companies Act Duties of Company Directors*.

Chapter 3

1. Alasdair MacIntyre (1988) *Whose Justice? Which Rationality* (Notre Dame, IL: University of Notre Dame Press).
2. Professors Tim Besley and Peter Hennessy (2009) Letter to HM Queen Elizabeth II, 22 July 2009, following the British Academy Forum "The Global Financial Crisis – Why Didn't Anybody Notice?".
3. Susan Strange (1986), *Casino Capitalism* (Oxford: Blackwell).
4. Goldman Sachs, *Code of Business Conduct and Ethics (Amended and Restated as of May 2009)*.

5. http://www2.goldmansachs.com/our-firm/our-people/business-principles.html, accessed 8 March 2011.
6. http://www2.goldmansachs.com/our-firm/investors/corporate-governance/corporate-governance-documents/revise-code-of-conduct.pdf, accessed 8 March 2011.
7. http://www.morganstanley.com/company/governance/pdf/codeofethicsweb version.pdf, accessed 8 March 2011.
8. http://www.nomuraholdings.com/company/basic/ethics.pdf, accessed 8 March 2011.

Chapter 4

1. Katinka C. van Cranenburgh, Daniel Arenas, Celine Louche, Jordi Vives (2010) *From Faith to Faith Consistent Investing* (3iG).
2. Benedict XVI (2009) *Caritas in Veritate*.
3. Rowan Williams and Larry Elliott (eds) (2010) *Crisis and Recovery* (London: Palgrave Macmillan).
4. http://www.churchofengland.org/about-us/structure/eiag/ethical-investment-policies.aspx, accessed 8 March 2011.
5. http://www.cfbmethodistchurch.org.uk/ethics/index.html, accessed 8 March 2011.
6. Rabbi Dr Asher Meir (2009) *Jewish Values Based Investment Guide* (Business Ethics Center of Jerusalem).
7. http://www.djindexes.com/mdsidx/html/pressrelease/press_hist2008.html#2008 0115, accessed 12 January 2010.
8. http://www.cofe.anglican.org/info/ethical/, accessed 7 September 2010.
9. http://www.cfbmethodistchurch.org.uk/downloads/policy_statements/cfb_alcohol_policy_statement.pdf, accessed 8 March 2011.

Chapter 5

1. The statements of Senator Levin and Mr Blankfein can be accessed at http://hsgac.senate.gov/public/index.cfm?FuseAction=Hearings.Hearing&Hearing_id=f07ef2 bf-914c-494c-aa66-27129f8e6282, accessed 8 March 2011.
2. http://www.sec.gov/news/press/2010/2010-59.htm, accessed 8 March 2011.

Chapter 6

1. http://www.sec.gov/news/press/2010/2010-59.htm, accessed 8 March 2011.
2. Russell Hotten, "Shell Plots $1.2 bn Regal Takeover Bid", *Daily Telegraph*, 2 October 2008, http://www.telegraph.co.uk/finance/newsbysector/energy/oilandgas/3124785/Shell-plots-1.2bn-Regal-takeover-bid.html, accessed 11 March 2011.
3. Rule 2.2 (c) of the Takeover Code states that an announcement is required "when following an approach to the offeree company, the offeree company is the subject of rumour and speculation or there is an untoward movement in its share price". The Panel on Takeovers and Mergers (2009) *The Takeover Code*, 9th edn.

4. http://fsahandbook.info/FSA/html/handbook/MAR/1, accessed 8 March 2011.
5. http://eur-lex.europa.eu/LexUriServ/site/en/oj/2003/l_336/l_33620031223en00 330038.pdf, accessed 8 March 2011.
6. *The Times*, 6 March 2010, http://business.timesonline.co.uk/tol/business/ economics/article7052224.ece, accessed 9 January 2011.
7. A. R. Paley and D. S. Hilzenrath "SEC Chief Defends His Restraint", *Washington Post*, 24 November 2008, http://www.washingtonpost.com/wp-dyn/content/ article/2008/12/23/AR2008122302765.html, accessed 8 March 2011.
8. R. Younglai, "SEC Chief has Regrets Over Short-Selling Ban," 31 December 2008, http://www.reuters.com/article/2008/12/31/us-sec-cox-idUSTRE4BU3GG2008 1231, accessed 8 March 2011.
9. Financial Services Authority (2009) Discussion Paper Short-Selling, http://www. fsa.gov.uk/pubs/discussion/dp09_01.pdf, accessed 8 March 2011.

Chapter 8

1. http://www.legislation.gov.uk/ukpga/2010/23/contents, accessed 8 March 2011.
2. Project Merlin – Banks' Statement (9 February 2011), http://www.hm-treasury. gov.uk/d/bank_agreement_090211.pdf, accessed 8 March 2011.
3. Richard Higginson and David Clough (2010) *The Ethics of Executive Remuneration: A Guide for Christian Investors* (Church Investors Group).

Bibliography

Abrahamson, M. (2009) "Conflicts of Interest in Investment Banking" (unpublished D.Phil. thesis, University of Oxford).

Aragon, G.A. (2011) *Financial Ethics: A Positivist Analysis* (New York: Oxford University Press).

Arestis, P., R. Sobreira and J.L. Oreiro (2011) *An Assessment of the Global Impact of the Financial Crisis* (Basingstoke: Palgrave Macmillan).

Arestis, P., R. Sobreira and J.L. Oreiro (2011) *The Financial Crisis: Origins and Implications* (Basingstoke and New York: Palgrave Macmillan).

Audi, R. (2009) *Business Ethics and Ethical Business* (New York and Oxford: Oxford University Press).

Ayub, M. (2007) *Understanding Islamic Finance* (Chichester: Wiley).

Banks, E. (2010) *See No Evil: Uncovering the Truth Behind the Financial Crisis* (Basingstoke: Palgrave Macmillan).

Benedict XVI (2009) Encyclical Letter, *Caritas in Veritate*

Besley, R. and P. Hennessy (2009) Letter to HM Queen Elizabeth II, 22 July 2009, following the British Academy Forum "The Global Financial Crisis – Why Didn't Anybody Notice?" http://www.britac.ac.uk/events/archive/forum-economy.cfm, accessed 12 May 2011.

Bibb, S. (2010) *The Right Thing to Do: An Everyday Guide to Ethics in Business* (Chichester: Wiley).

Bibb, S. and J. Kourdi (2007) *A Question of Trust: The Crucial Nature of Trust in Business, Work and Life and How to Build It* (London: Cyan).

Blackburn, S. (2001) *Being Good: An Introduction to Ethics* (Oxford: Oxford University Press).

Boatright, J.R. (2010), *Finance Ethics: Critical Issues in Theory and Practice* (Hoboken, NJ: Wiley).

Bootle, R. (2009) *The Trouble with Markets* (London and Boston: Nicholas Brealey Publishing).

Bradburn, R. (2001) *Understanding Business Ethics* (London and New York: Continuum).

Brown, G. (2010) *Beyond the Crash: Overcoming the First Crisis of Globalisation* (London: Simon & Schuster).

Buckley, A. (2011) *Financial Crisis: Causes, Context and Consequences* (Harlow and New York: Financial Times/Prentice Hall).

Cassell, C., P. Johnson and K. Smith (1997) "Opening the Black Box: Corporate Codes of Ethics in their Organisational Context", *Journal of Business Ethics*, 16, 1077–93.

Chakraborty, S.K. (1996) *Ethics in Management: Vedantic Perspectives* (Delhi: Oxford University Press).

Chen, A.Y.S., R.B. Sawyers and P.F. Williams (1997) "Reinforcing Ethical Decision Making Through Corporate Culture", *Journal of Business Ethics*, 16, 855–65.

Childs, J.M. (2000) *Greed: Economics and Ethics in Conflict* (Minneapolis, MN: Fortress Press).

Christie, P.M.J., I.-W.G. Kwon, P.A. Stoeberl and R. Baumhart (2003) "A Cross-Cultural Comparison of Ethical Attitudes of Business Managers: India, Korea and the United States", *Journal of Business Ethics,* 46 (3), 263–87.

Chryssides, G. and J.H. Kaler (1996) *Essentials of Business Ethics* (London: McGraw Hill).

Collier, J. (1995) "The Virtuous Organization" *Business Ethics: A European Review,* 4 (3), 143–9.

Collins, J.W. (1994) "Is Business Ethics an Oxymoron?", *Business Horizons,* September–October, 1–8.

Crane, A. and D. Matten (2010) *Business Ethics: Managing Corporate Citizenship and Sustainability in the Age of Globalization,* 3rd edn (Oxford: Oxford University Press).

Crockett, A. (2003) *Conflicts of Interest in the Financial Services Industry: What Should We Do About Them?* (London: Centre for Economic Policy Research).

Crouch, C. and D. Marquand (eds) (1993) *Ethics and Markets: Co-operation and Competition Within Capitalist Economies* (Oxford: Blackwell).

Davies, H. (2010) *The Financial Crisis: Who is to Blame?* (Cambridge: Polity Press).

De George, R.T. (1999) *Business Ethics,* 5th edn (Upper Saddle River, NJ: Prentice Hall).

Deigh, J. (2010) *An Introduction to Ethics* (Cambridge: Cambridge University Press).

Dewatripont, M., J.-C. Rochet, J. Tirole and K. Tribe (2010) *Balancing the Banks: Global Lessons from the Financial Crisis* (Princeton and Oxford: Princeton University Press).

Dobos, N., C. Barry and T.W.M. Pogge (eds) (2011) *Global Financial Crisis: The Ethical Issues* (Basingstoke: Palgrave Macmillan).

Donaldson, T. (2008) "Hedge Fund Ethics", *Business Ethics Quarterly,* 18 (3), 405–16.

Ferrell, O.C., J. Fraedrich and L. Ferrell (2002) *Business Ethics: Ethical Decision Making and Cases,* 5th edn (Boston, MA: Houghton Mifflin).

Financial Services Authority (2009) Discussion Paper Short-Selling.

Fisher, C. and A. Lovell (2008) *Business Ethics and Values: Individual, Corporate and International Perspectives,* 3rd edn (Harlow: Financial Times/Prentice Hall).

Frederick, R. (ed.) (1999) *A Companion to Business Ethics* (Oxford: Blackwell).

Friedman, J. (ed.) (2011) *What Caused the Financial Crisis* (Philadelphia: University of Pennsylvania Press).

Fukuyama, F. (1996) *Trust: The Social Virtues and the Creation of Prosperity* (London: Penguin).

Gibson, K. (2007) *Ethics and Business: An Introduction* (Cambridge: Cambridge University Press).

Goldman Sachs (2009) *Code of Business Conduct and Ethics.*

Goodhart, C.A.E. (2009) *The Regulatory Response to the Financial Crisis* (Cheltenham and Northampton, MA: Edward Elgar).

Green, R.M. (1994) *The Ethical Manager: A New Method for Business Ethics* (Eaglewood, NJ: Macmillan).

Green, S. (2009) *Good Value: Reflections on Money, Morality and an Uncertain World* (London: Allen Lane).

Griffiths, B. (1982) *Morality and the Market Place* (London: Hodder and Stoughton).

Griffiths, B. (2001) *Capitalism, Morality and Markets* (London: Institute of Economic Affairs).

Griseri, T. (2010) *Business Ethics* (London: Cengage Learning).

Harries, R. (1995) *Questioning Belief* (London: SPCK).

Harvard Business School (2003) *Harvard Business Review on Corporate Ethics* (Cambridge, MA: Harvard Business School Press).

Hassan, K. and M. Lewis (eds) (2007) *Islamic Finance* (Cheltenham: Edward Elgar).

Henn, S.K. (2009) *Business Ethics: A Case Study Approach* (Hoboken, NJ: Wiley)

Higginson, R. and D. Clough (2010) *Ethics of Executive Pay: A Christian Viewpoint* (Cambridge: Grove).

Higginson, R. and D. Clough (2010) *The Ethics of Executive Remuneration: A Guide for Christian Investors* (Church Investors Group).

Higgs-Kleyn, N. and D. Kapeliansis (1999) "The Role of Professional Codes in Regulating Ethical Conduct", *Journal of Business Ethics*, 19, 363–74.

Hill, A. (1998) *Just Business: Christian Ethics for the Market Place* (Carlisle: Paternoster Press).

Hotten, R. (2008) "Shell Plots \$1.2 bn Regal Takeover Bid", *Daily Telegraph*, 2 October. http://www.telegraph.co.uk/finance/newsbysector/energy/oilandgas/3124785/Shell-plots-1.2bn-Regal-takeover-bid.html, accessed 12 May 2011.

Howes, S., and P. Robins (1994) *A Theory of Moral Organization: A Buddhist View of Business Ethics* (Birmingham: Aston Business School Research Institute).

Independent Banking Commission (2010) *Issues Paper Call for Evidence.*

Jones, C., M. Parker and R. ten Bos (2005) *For Business Ethics: A Critical Approach* (London: Routledge).

Jones, I. and M. Pollitt (eds) (1998) *The Role of Business Ethics in Economic Performance* (London: Macmillan).

Kline, J.M. (2005) *Ethics for International Business: Decision Making in a Global Political Economy* (London: Routledge).

Koehn, D. (1999) "What Can Eastern Philosophy Teach Us About Business Ethics?", *Journal of Business Ethics*, 19, 71–9.

Koslowski, P. (2011) *The Ethics of Banking: Conclusions from the Financial Crisis* (Dordrecht, Heidelberg, London, New York: Springer).

Leeson, N.W. with E. Whitley (1997) *Rogue Trader* (London: Warner).

Levine, A. (1980) *Free Enterprise and Jewish Law: Aspects of Jewish Business Ethics* (New York: Yeshiva University Press).

Lewis, M. (2010) *The Big Short* (London and New York: Allen Lane/W. W. Norton).

Liaw, K.T. (2006) *The Business of Investment Banking: A Comprehensive Overview*, 2nd edn (Hoboken, NJ: Wiley).

Lynch, J.L. (1994) *Banking and Finance: Managing the Moral Dimension* (Cambridge: Gresham/Woodhead).

MacIntyre, A. (1984) *After Virtue: A Study in Moral Theory* (Notre Dame, IL: University of Notre Dame Press).

McCloskey, D.N. (2006) *The Bourgeois Virtues: Ethics for an Age of Commerce* (Chicago: University of Chicago Press).

McCosh, A.M. (1999) *Financial Ethics* (Boston, MA: Klewer Academic Publishers).

McEwan, T. (2001) *Managing Values and Beliefs in Organisations* (Harlow: Pearson Education).

McLemore, C.W. (2003) *Street-Smart Ethics: Succeeding in Business Without Selling Your Soul* (Louisville and London: Westminster John Knox Press).

Megone, C. and S. J. Robinson (eds) (2002) *Case Histories in Business Ethics* (London and New York: Routledge).

Meir, A. (2009) *Jewish Values Based Investment Guide* (Business Ethics Center of Jerusalem).

Melé, D. (2009) *Business Ethics in Action* (Basingstoke: Palgrave Macmillan).

Messer, N. (2006) *SCM Studyguide to Christian Ethics* (London: SCM).

Moon, C. and C. Bonny (eds) (2001) *Business Ethics: Facing up to the Issues* (London: Economist Books).

Moore, D.A. (ed.) (2005) *Conflicts of Interest: Challenges and Solutions in Business, Law, Medicine, and Public Policy* (Cambridge: Cambridge University Press).

Moore, J. (1990) "What is Really Unethical about Insider Trading?", *Journal of Business Ethics*, 9, 171–82.

Morris, D. (2004) "Defining a Moral Problem in Business Ethics", *Journal of Business Ethics*, 49, 347–57.

Newton, A. (1998) *Compliance: Making Ethics Work in Financial Services* (London: Pitman).

Nyaw, M.-K. and I. Ng (1994) "A Comparative Analysis of Ethical Beliefs: A Four Country Study", *Journal of Business Ethics*, 13 (7), 543–55.

Oakley, J. and D. Cocking (2001) *Virtue Ethics and Professional Roles* (Cambridge: Cambridge University Press).

O'Brien, T. and S. Paeth (eds) (2007) *Religious Perspectives on Business Ethics: An Anthology* (Lanham, MD and Plymouth: Rowman & Littlefield).

O'Neill, O. (2002) *A Question of Trust* (Cambridge: Cambridge University Press).

Paley, A.R. and D.S. Hilzenrath (2008) "SEC Chief Defends His Restraint", *Washington Post*, 24 November, http://www.washingtonpost.com/wp-dyn/content/article/2008/12/23/AR2008122302765.html, accessed 8 March 2011.

Pava, M.L. (1998) "The Substance of Jewish Business Ethics", *Journal of Business Ethics*, 17 (6), 603–17.

Premeaux, S.R. and R.W. Mondy (1993) "Linking Management Behavior to Ethical Philosophy", *Journal of Business Ethics*, 12, 349–57.

Rawls, J. (1971) *A Theory of Justice* (Cambridge, MA: Harvard University Press).

Reynolds, J. (2010) "Investment Banking: The Inevitable Triumph of Incentives over Ethics", in R. Williams and L. Elliott (eds) *Crisis and Recovery* (London: Palgrave Macmillan).

Rider, B., K. Alexander and L. Linklater (2007) *Market Abuse and Insider Dealing* (Haywards Heath: Tottel).

Rosenthal, S.B. and R.A. Buchholz (2000) *Rethinking Business Ethics: A Pragmatic Approach* (New York and Oxford: Oxford University Press).

Sadeq, AH.M. and K. Ahmad (eds) (2001) *Ethics in Business and Management: Islamic and Mainstream Approaches* (London: Asean Academic Press).

Schwartz, M. (2000) "Why Ethical Codes Constitute an Unconscionable Regression", *Journal of Business Ethics*, 23, 173–84.

Seldon, A. (2009) *Trust: How We Lost it and How to Get it Back* (London: Biteback).

Singer, P. (ed.) (1991) *A Companion to Ethics* (Oxford: Blackwell).

Sinn, H.-W. (2010) *Casino Capitalism: How the Financial Crisis Came about and What Needs to be Done Now* (Oxford: Oxford University Press).

Smith, A. (1759) *The Theory of Moral Sentiments*.

Smith, A. (1776) *The Wealth of Nations* (London: W. Strahan and T. Cadell).

Sorkin, A.R. (2009) *Too Big to Fail: The Inside Story of How Wall Street and Washington Fought to Save the Financial System from Crisis – and Themselves* (New York: Viking).

Stackhouse, M.L. (2001) "Business, Economics and Christian Ethics", in R. Gill (ed.) *The Cambridge Companion to Christian Ethics* (Cambridge: Cambridge University Press).

Stackhouse, M.L., D.P. McCann, S.J. Roels with P.N. Williams (1995) *On Moral Business: Classical and Contemporary Resources for Ethics in Economic Life* (Grand Rapids, MI: Eerdmans).

Stanwick, P.A. and S.D. Stanwick (2009) *Understanding Business Ethics* (Upper Saddle River, NJ: Pearson/Prentice Hall).

Sternberg, E. (2000) *Just Business: Business Ethics in Action*, 2nd edn (Oxford: Oxford University Press).

Stiglitz, J.E. (2010) *Freefall: Free Markets and the Sinking of the Global Economy* (London: Penguin).

Strange, S. (1986) *Casino Capitalism* (Oxford: Blackwell).

Sullivan, R. (ed.) (2003) *Business and Human Rights: Dilemmas and Solutions* (Sheffield: Greenleaf).

Taylor, M.P. and R.H. Clarida (2011) *The Global Financial Crisis* (London: Routledge).

Thomsen, S., C. Rose and O. Risager (2009) *Understanding the Financial Crisis: Investment, Risk and Governance* (Copenhagen: SimCorp).

Ulrich, P. (2008) *Integrative Economic Ethics: Foundations of a Civilized Market Economy* (Cambridge: Cambridge University Press).

van Cranenburgh, K.C., D. Arenas, C. Louche and J. Vives (2010) *From Faith to Faith Consistent Investing* (3iG).

Velasquez, M.G. (1998) *Business Ethics: Concepts and Cases*, 4th edn (Upper Saddle River, NJ: Prentice Hall).

Verstraeten, J. (ed.) (2000) *Business Ethics: Broadening the Perspectives* (Leuven: Peters).

Wang, W.K.S. and M.I. Steinberg (2010) *Insider Trading*, 3rd edn (New York and Oxford: Oxford University Press).

Webley, S. (ed.) (2008) *Use of Codes of Ethics in Business: 2007 Survey and Analysis of Trends* (London: Institute of Business Ethics).

Webley, S. and M. Le Jeune (2005) *Corporate Use of Codes of Ethics: 2004 Survey* (London: Institute of Business Ethics).

Wienen, I. (1999) *Impact of Religion on Business Ethics in Europe and the Muslim World: Islamic versus Christian Tradition* (Oxford: Peter Lang).

Williams, R. and L. Elliott (eds) (2010) *Crisis and Recovery* (London: Palgrave Macmillan).

Wright, C. (2004) *The Business of Virtue* (London: SPCK).

Younglai, R. (2008) "SEC Chief has Regrets over Short-selling Ban", 31 December, http://www.reuters.com/article/2008/12/31/us-sec-cox-idUSTRE4BU3GG20081231, accessed 8 March 2011.

Zsolnai, L. (2011) *Spirituality and Ethics in Management* (Dordrecht, Heidelberg, London, New York: Springer).

Index